11·95

74523

1/12/98

FO...

THE CHINESE ECONOMY

Published by Economica Ltd.
9 Wimpole Street
London W1M 8LB

© Economica Ltd., 1998

First published 1998

Printed in France

Michel Fouquin & Françoise Lemoine, Editors

The Chinese Economy
Highlights & Opportunities

ISBN 1-902282-03-5

Michel FOUQUIN
& Françoise LEMOINE
editors

The Chinese Economy

Highlights and Opportunities

ECONOMICA
London • Paris • Genève

Acknowledgements

The first exporter among developing countries and the main host for foreign direct investment after the United States in 1996, China is at last modernising itself at great speed. The CEPII and its company club the CIREM thus chose to organise an international conference in order to draw together the available information concerning China's growth, its reforms and its relations with its neighbours. This conference brought together experts from various professional horizons: academics and researchers, bankers and industrialists, international civil servants were therefore able to contrast their analyses and experiences.

Chance would have it that the conference took place in Paris a few days before the first symptoms of the Asian financial crisis came out into the open, a crisis which is a key moment in the contemporary economic history of the region. It is therefore more necessary than ever before to evaluate the real economic potential of China, and the organisers of the conference hope that the publication of its proceedings will contribute to this debate.

The CEPII and the CIREM would like to thank the Compagnie Financière Edmond de Rothschild, Air France, and the newspaper *Le Monde* for their support in organising the conference, as well as the French Ministry of Education and Research which hosted the meeting.

Marie-Pierre Mol, Secretary-General of the CIREM, played a pivotal role in organising the conference, as well as in collecting and preparing the papers presented; Nicholas Sowels translated them; and Véronique le Rolland prepared and typeset the manuscript.

This publication is to be the CEPII's first in a series of books in English. The Centre is collaborating with the Economica publishing house and the Brookings Institution to ensure a wide distribution of its works in English, which should allow the CEPII, France's primary research institute specialising in international economics, to deepen its links with international research networks in economics.

Contents

Introduction

By Michel FOUQUIN[*]
and Françoise LEMOINE[**]

At a time when financial turmoil is devastating East Asia, China, and countries or territories whose populations are made up of a majority of ethnic Chinese (Hong Kong, Taiwan and Singapore) look like a sea of calm and prosperity. Is this an illusion?

In fact, one has to be very cautious when trying to assess the soundness of economic performance, as well as evaluating the economic value of a bank or an industrial firm. We have learned the hard way—and very recently in the Korean case (or even in the Japanese case)—that basic macro-economic indicators as well as micro-economic data (firm level data) can hide some crucial aspects of reality if taken at face value. Without being as cynical as some economists are, we do not consider statistical data as only a sophisticated way of lying for politicians. The quality of data is necessary both for correct decision-making and for correct assessment by investors. Bad quality data may have very high economic costs in terms of wrong decisions or in terms of risk premia.

China is probably one of the most troublesome countries as far as economic information is concerned. As a result, experts are divided on almost every aspect of the country. The size of the country which defies any generalisation, the level of development and five decades of communist leadership, who can be seen as masters in the art of manipulating information, are three major reasons for explaining the widely diverging views about the country's past, present and future. So one may question the use of experts, if only because they add noise to a complex and transitory situation. We believe, nevertheless, that it is possible to elaborate some consensus on important issues. This book is part of many efforts which are made to improve our knowledge about China, though it clearly does not pretend to put forward the complete truth.

COMPARING GROWTH AND WELFARE

If we stick to official data, they indicate that China's economic performance, since the beginning of economic reform in 1979, has been among the highest in the world. International investors have plebiscited the country, and their investments amount to levels second only to foreign investment in the

[*] Deputy Director of the CEPII; [**] senior economist at the CEPII; written in May 1998.

USA, for 1995 and 1996. Yet, most experts now agree that Chinese economic growth is over-estimated. This is due, principally, to the fact that inflation is under-estimated. Real growth, since 1978, has probably been closer to 7%, rather than to 9%, which is the official evaluation.

Short-comings in the Chinese statistics also appear when one tries to measure the average standard of living of the Chinese people, and to make a comparison with other countries. Real per capita wealth, as approximated by Gross Domestic Product per capita at current exchange rates, is grossly under-estimated, probably by a factor of four or five (the latter being the maximum). The reasons behind such a mis-measurement are twofold: first, the Chinese data under-estimate the level of output as they inadequately cover service and private sector activities. The second reason is the under-valuation of the currency, known as the Balassa effect. Developing countries are supposed to be relatively less efficient (productive) in manufacturing industries than in services, activities which are protected from international competition. Under-valuation is supposed to correct the relative weakness of developing countries in manufacturing activities, which is revealed by their higher domestic prices. If exchange rates based on Purchasing Power Parity are used, then the Chinese standard of living was superior to US$ 2000 in 1990. Consequently, China is already one of the major economic powers of the world, with a GNP roughly equal to twice the British GNP.

NOT SO PRODUCTIVE

In China, the source of economic growth since 1978 has been first capital accumulation, second productivity growth, and third labour force expansion. Productivity gains amount to a major success of the Chinese economy. But the reallocation of labour from agriculture to industry has contributed to a large extent to the progress made. Before the economic reforms, the share of primary activities—mostly agriculture— in employment was very high and stable. Since then, the shares of industry and services have increased steadily. As the value-added per worker in industry is at least twice that of agriculture, structural change has led to higher productivity. When looking at the gap between global productivity in the manufacturing sector in developed countries and China, it seems that the relative progress made by China is close to zero. This result is consistent with the findings of economists like A. Young, who found that the Asian Tigers' performance was explained well by their huge amounts of physical capital investment, rather than by an improvement in their overall productive efficiency. However, such estimates are based on the value of the residuals of weak statistics, and depend on production functions that are themselves subject to controversy, leaving room for some scepticism. In particular, most studies are based on the hypothesis of a fixed share of production factors over time. This is acceptable for industrialised countries, but not for rapidly emerging countries such as China.

NOT SO OPEN

Another consequence of under-valuation is that the rate of openness of the Chinese economy as measured by the ratio of exported goods to GNP is around 4%, rather than the 20% put forward by the official figures; the difference comes from the fact that products which are exported or imported are valued at international prices, whereas domestic value added is evaluated at domestic prices and is therefore undervalued.

Furthermore, around 40% of exports are produced by joint-ventures, which are located in coastal provinces and benefit from special treatment (such as the free entry of capital equipment and intermediate goods on the condition that their products are exported). Access to the domestic market remains rather limited and openness to trade is still low. One of the major reasons for the high barriers to the domestic market is the existence of a highly inefficient, state-owned enterprise sector. The 15th session of the Central Committee in September 1997 chose to accelerate dramatically the reform of this sector as a priority. The detailed policy is still not clear, but it will be a major step for China.

CHAOTIC REFORM PROCESS

If statistical information is difficult to interpret, then what can be said of the economic and political reform process in China? The best way to assess this is probably to look at the real consequences of reforms, rather than to the explanations given by political leaders.

As far as reforms are concerned, they follow a highly pragmatic process. China is opening up, undoubtedly, but the rhythm is rather slow and the process chaotic. It is a kind of trial-and-error approach. China is still a country managed by a Communist Party whose long and glorious revolutionary history makes it difficult to recognise officially that its economic model is that of a kind of capitalist economy. The official slogan of "a market economy under socialist command" may sound like a Braudelian slogan, as Braudel made a clear distinction between the market economy and capitalism. The market economy is an economy of small markets, in which an infinite number of producers sell their products to an infinite number of customers, and the market is the basis of the economy. Capitalism then appears when there is a strong concentration of economic power in the hands of a limited number of people, located in a specific territory, such as Venice, Genoa or Amsterdam. Under a capitalist system, bankers, international traders, big corporations and the State dominate the national economy. The rules that regulate the capitalist system are those of power games, and of military strategy, not those of the market. The theoretical backgrounds of the capitalism are those of Sun Tsé, rather than of Adam Smith, those of warfare rather than marketfare.

The Japanese model is to some extent a good illustration of this kind of system, which was nicknamed **Japan Inc**. Japan has tried to popularise its system through the financial and intellectual support for the World Bank's famous study on "Southeast Asian Miracles".

Socialist China is clearly trying to develop its own variety of the model, due to its specific history and problems as a potential world power. In looking for a Chinese model, it is probably more interesting to look to Taiwan rather than to Korea, in spite of the fact that the new Chinese Prime Minister has made specific references to the *chaebol* system (the Korean name for Korean conglomerates) in his introduction to the reform of state-owned enterprises.

Taiwan has been dominated by a single Party, the Kuomintang, whose members were Mainland Chinese. Public monopolies were in the hands of the Party, as were many big firms. Since the economic reforms of the late fifties, the Taiwanese people have been developing their own small, family-type businesses, which have become the core of Taiwan's successes in the world markets.

The evolution of the mainland industry could follow a similar path: big firms could stay in the hands of the Chinese government, while small businesses could become the basis of truly free, capitalist and family-type enterprises.

Another argument in favour of the Taiwanese model is the fact that foreign direct investment plays an important role in Taiwan, and no role in Korea (the same is true for Japan). In Mainland China, foreign direct investment is already playing a strategic role in the export industry and in some other industries.

Last but not least, Korea now faces a major crisis, which is challenging the relevance of its model, in the face of globalisation. In contrast, Taiwan is proving to be more immune to financial crisis.

CHINA AND THE CURRENT ECONOMIC CRISIS: TWO SCENARIOS FOR THE FUTURE

The crisis in East Asia is said to be the crisis of the Asian development model. This model is said to be based on strong and incestuous relations between the State, industrial firms and the banking system. The State has the power to decide which industry is to be a strategic industry, to channel financial funds towards the industry, to import adequate technologies, and to support the creation of big enterprises which are supposed to attain world standards of efficiency and to compete in international markets through economies of scale and a learning process protected by high barriers.

China is facing some of the major problems of other Asian countries: inefficient enterprises, quasi-bankrupt banks supporting deficient state-owned firms, over-capacity of production in many sectors such as the consumer electronics industry, the automotive industry, and non-residential construction to name but a few.

But, from a macro-economic point of view, China has realised major accomplishments: inflation has been reduced to zero, its financial reserves are among the highest in the world, and China's exports are still (in 1998) very competitive (its exports to the US and Europe in the first quarter of 1998 grew by more than 20% and 30% respectively, over last year).

The two faces of China are paradoxical. Two scenarios are therefore plausible.

The first scenario is based on the idea that China is loosing its competitive advantage. The decline of Chinese competitiveness, due to the fall of other Asian currencies, leads to a very rapid decrease in export growth, which will dramatically reduce the level of official currency reserves and then necessitate a drastic adjustment of the Remnibi exchange rate. This could have incalculable consequences on the regional crisis and start a new round of financial turmoil. The cost for China and other Asian countries could be very large for a whole decade.

The second scenario is based on the idea the Chinese advantage in competitiveness was so huge before the crisis that it can afford reduced growth in its export sector, a reduced trade surplus and even a small deficit. Increased external investment would result from the privatisation process, and domestic-led growth would stem from allowing average-income households to use their huge savings to buy their homes. This scenario would help the region to adjust to reduced competition from China. The political as well as economic benefits for China would be very substantial.

For most experts the difficult period for East Asia is the year 1998, which will show whether the adjustment process is going in the right direction. The major source of weakness in Asia is probably Japan, both due to the fact that Japan cannot financially support the other countries in difficulty, and that its growth cannot be the engine pulling the regional economy out of recession, as the US economy did for Mexico.

But, after a period of stabilisation, the second scenario nevertheless seems more plausible.

PART 1

Assessing China's Economic Performance and Reforms

CHAPTER 1
CHINESE ECONOMIC PERFORMANCE IN HISTORICAL AND COMPARATIVE PERSPECTIVE

Angus MADDISON [*]

When putting Chinese performance into comparative and historical perspective, trying to clarify the reasons why growth accelerated so much in the Reform period, and explaining why, in the communist period as a whole, performance was totally different from past history, five main topics deserve emphasis.

1. MEASURING THE GROWTH RATE REALISTICALLY

The first major point is to get a valid comparative measure of growth and of levels of performance. The official Chinese estimates exaggerate growth and they understate the level of performance. Consequently certain components of Chinese GDP have to be reestimated: agriculture, industry and those service activities not included in the statistics before 1978 (see Table 1).

My new estimates for agriculture show slightly faster growth than the official Chinese estimates, considerably slower growth for industry and non-productive services which are the main sectors where inflation is underestimated. The overall impact of the adjustment is a growth rate for the Reform period of 7.4 % a year rather than the official 9.8%, and for the Maoist period a rate of 4.4% instead of 6% in the official figures.

2. MEASURING THE LEVEL OF PERFORMANCE REALISTICALLY

The other important question is to estimate the level of Chinese income. If you take the official GDP in yuan and convert it into dollars at the exchange rate (4.78 yuan to the dollar), you get 387 billion US dollars for GDP in my benchmark year 1990.

---

[*] Professor Emeritus, Groningen University.

Table 1 : Confrontation of Official and Maddison Measures of Growth Performance

	Official Measures		Maddison Measures	
	1952-78	1978-94	1952-78	1978-94
GDP	6.0	9.8	4.4	7.4
Population	2.0	1.4	2.0	1.4
Per Capita GDP	3.9	8.3	2.3	6.0
Employment	2.5	2.7	2.6	2.7
Labour Productivity	3.2	7.0	1.8	4.6
Agriculture (Farming, Forestry, Fishery and Sidelines)				
Value Added	1.9	5.1	2.2	
Per Capita V.A.	-0.2	3.7	0.2	
Employment	2.0	1.0	2.0	
Labour Productivity	-0.2	4.1	0.2	
Industry (Mining, Manufacturing and Utilities)				
Value Added	11.4	11.9	9.6	
Per Capita V.A.	9.2	10.4	7.4	
Employment	6.0	3.6	6.0	
Labour Productivity	5.1	8.0	3.3	
« Non-productive » Services				
Value Added	n.a.	11.9	4.2	
Per Capita V.A.	n.a.	10.3	1.5	
Employment	4,2	6.7	4.2	
Labour Productivity	n.a.	4.9	0.0	

Source: Official figures of real output for 1952-78 use the old concept of net material product which was borrowed from Soviet statistical practice.   It excluded some services considered non-productive as well as depreciation. For 1978 onwards the Chinese authorities have provided estimates which in theory conform to Western national accounting practice.

The purchasing power estimates show that you could buy a US dollar's worth of goods for less than 1 yuan. With the Purchasing Power Parity (PPP) converter one arrives at a 1990 Chinese GDP which is about five times larger.

With an 11% further upward adjustment of the yuan value, which I believe to be necessary to correct for official understatement, my estimate of Chinese GDP in dollars is 2.1 trillion for 1990 (see Table 2).

Table 2: Growth and Level of GDP, Population and GDP per Capita, Benchmark
Years China 1820-1994

	GDP Index (1913=100.00)	GDP level (million 1987 Yuan)	GDP level (million 1990 int. $)	Population (000s)	Per capita GDP(1990 int. $)
1820	90.70	156,557	219,075	381,000	575
1890	85.10	146,836	205,472	380,000	541
1913	100.00	172,611	241,540	437,140	553
1933	119.80	206,838	289,434	500,000	579
1952	126.70	218,670	305,991	568,910	538
1957	168.60	291,033	407,251	637,408	639
1978	386.70	667,554	934,127	956,165	977
1987	764.30	1,319,275	1, 846,098	1, 084,035	1,703
1990	871.70	1,504,591	2 ,105,416	1, 135,185	1,855
1994	1,219.60	2,105,231	2 ,945,908	1, 191,835	2,472

Source: A. Maddison, *Chinese Economic Performance in the Long run*, OECD,
Paris 1998.

In January 1997, Christopher Patten, then governor of Hong-Kong,
wrote an article in *The Economist* in which he said "Britain's GDP today is
almost twice the size of China's. China's GDP is about the same as those of
Belgium, Netherlands and Luxembourg combined". This kind of statement is
extremely misleading. With the PPP converter Chinese GDP is about 7 times as
big as that of Belgium, Netherlands and Luxembourg combined and 3 times as
big as that of the UK.

The foreign trade ratio is a further illustration of the importance of
using the right conversion. The normally quoted figure is that China exports
about 20 % of its GDP but if you use the PPP converter Chinese exports are only
4% of GDP.

Purchasing power parity estimates make an enormous difference to the
way you measure Chinese performance. It is normal in a developing country to
find that the PPP is very different from the exchange rate. You find this for India
though the difference is not so extreme as in China. For international
comparison, it is much better to use the PPP converter than the exchange rate.
Otherwise you get an assessment of the Chinese situation which is totally
misleading.

It is important to put Chinese GDP in a world perspective. With the
PPP conversion, China is now the second biggest country, after the USA. By the
year 2015, if you extrapolate Chinese growth at slightly less than it has been
achieving, i.e. at 6% and American growth at 2.5 %, the Chinese GDP will be
bigger than that of the USA. Another thing which is interesting in geopolitical

terms is the relationship between Chinese GDP and Soviet or Russian GDP (see Table 3).

In 1978, when the Reform period began, Chinese aggregate GDP was about 54% of Soviet GDP. In the meantime the Soviet Union has disappeared, Russia has 143 million people less than the Soviet Union, and Russian GDP per head has fallen by a third, so Chinese GDP is now more than 4 times as big as Russian GDP. This is worth keeping in mind when considering the way China should be treated, for instance in joining the WTO. It is not a little country you can push around easily without dangerous consequences.

There is another important point to note about Chinese per capita growth (Table 3). Between 1820 and 1952 Chinese per capita GDP declined. In the same period, US per capita GDP increased 8 fold, Europe's GDP increased 4-fold and Japan's 3 fold. Consequently China's position deteriorated a lot. In the Maoist period, China increased its GDP per head about 80 % and in the Reform period about 2.5 times. China is now in a golden age of economic growth and you have to go back to the Sung dynasty, between the 10th and the 13th century, to find previous evidence of substantial increase of Chinese per capita GDP. What's happening in China is quite an historic change. In the Reform period, China has definitely been one of the super-growth countries, even if you use my estimates, which are lower than the official ones.

3. UNDERSTANDING THE NATURE OF PERFORMANCE IN THE MAOIST PERIOD

What caused this acceleration during the communist period compared with the long run? In the Maoist period (1952-1978) there was a major effort at resource mobilisation and accumulation, which was possible because the Chinese communist government was very strong compared to previous governments. By squeezing the consumption share, and transferring property rights to the State, it managed to raise the rate of fixed non-residential investment from around 4% in pre-war years to around 16 % of GDP. This is lower than Chinese official statistics show because they used a concept of "accumulation" which was total investment divided by "net material product" (the denominator was too low). Also, "accumulation" included very large investment in inventories, much higher than in western countries or in Japan. In the Reform period, investment in inventories averaged 6.8% of GDP, whereas in Japan it was 0.5 % of GDP and in some European countries less than that.

Labour input also increased relative to population. The activity rate rose from 36% to 42% of the population in 1952-1978.

Table 3: Comparative Levels of Economic Performance, China and Other Major Parts of the World Economy, 1820-1994

	China	Japan	Europe	Russia	India	World
GDP (billion 1990 « international » dollars)						
1820	219.1	21.8	187.7	33.8	110.0	714.7
1890	205.5	39.0	629.7	99.0	171.0	1,559.9
1913	241.5	68.9	996.6	229.2	201.1	2,666.7
1933	289.4	137.2	1,181.3	236.9	227.4	3,304.4
1952	306.0	196.5	1,723.6	512.6	226.6	5,892.4
1978	934.1	1,400.4	5,216.4	1,715.2	630.8	18,611.5
1994	2,945.9	2,407.8	7,004.0	675.7	1,319.6	29,191.9
Population (million)						
1820	381	31	167	45	209	1,068
1890	380	40	271	107	281	1,451
1913	437	52	327	154	304	1,772
1933	500	67	362	159	350	2,136
1952	569	86	402	186	372	2,606
1978	956	115	481	261	649	4,263
1994	1,192	125	505	150	900	5,613
GDP capita (1990 « international » dollars)						
1820	575	704	1,123	751	531	669
1890	541	974	2,324	925	608	1,075
1913	553	1,334	3,044	1,488	663	1,505
1933	579	2,042	3,260	1,493	649	1,547
1952	538	2,277	4,287	2,928	609	2,261
1978	977	12,186	10,851	6,565	972	4,366
1994	2,472	19,269	13,879	4,265	1,446	5,201

Source: A. Maddison, *Chinese Economic Performance in the Long Run*, OECD, Paris, 1998

These are two major elements which led to faster growth, but the payoff on investment, and increased labour input was limited because production was concentrated in overlarge enterprises. The most striking example of that is the period of the great leap forward when the Chinese farm sector which previously had over 100 million farms was suddenly concentrated into 26,000 farms. Average farm size in terms of employment was 30 times as big as Soviet collective or state farms.

Chinese industrial enterprises were also too big to be run efficiently although they were quite a lot smaller than Soviet enterprises. In 1978, the average Chinese industrial enterprise employed 175 people whereas the average Soviet enterprise employed 800 people. In the US the average industrial enterprise employed less than 60 people. Of course the USA had very big firms but it had proportionally many more small firms than China or the USSR.

Some of this inefficiency was characteristic of all socialist command economies but the great leap forward and other erratic changes in policy made inefficiency worse.

There was very little use of market processes. There was an extreme isolation from world trade which was not voluntary. In a first place, China got aid from the Soviet Union but they quarrelled, and in the 1960s this trade almost disappeared. At the same time, the US had imposed a total trade embargo on China from Korean War until 1971. The degree of isolation of China in the post-war period was hence very unusual in terms of trade, foreign investment and transfers of technology.

The great leap forward caused the biggest damage, but the Cultural Revolution led to a virtual shutdown of all higher and secondary technical education.

So you had a respectable degree of resource mobilisation but a somewhat worse allocation of resources than in an average Soviet-type economy.

4. EXPLAINING THE IMPROVED PERFORMANCE OF THE REFORM PERIOD

In the Golden Age after 1978, there was an increase in the average rate of fixed non-residential investment to 21% of GDP compared to 16% in the Maoist period. A significant part of that investment was financed by private savings and its allocation was more efficient. Labour input again increased. Chinese employment is now around 52% of the whole population, which is very high by any standards. In terms of efficiency, there has been a dramatic decentralisation and downsizing of enterprises. In agriculture, the average production unit in 1978 was the production team which involved on average 34 people. Now the typical unit is the family farm which employs on average 1.4 people. In industry, the production unit used to be an average of 175 people in 1978 in 348.000 enterprises. There are now over 7 million industrial enterprises, and on average they employ 15 persons. In commerce and restaurants, there has been a very big increase in activity (this sector was squeezed in the Maoist period). In 1995, there were 15.8 million enterprises compared to 1.2 million in 1978. The average size of these enterprises is now 2.3 persons rather than 4.7. In all these new enterprises incentives for work are better, resource allocation is considerably improved, and there have been sizeable productivity gains. In agriculture, the labour productivity gain has been about 4% a year. In industry, the productivity growth is much faster in the smaller enterprises than in the state enterprises.

The other thing which is important is the opening of the economy to the international trade. This is a big change compared to the Maoist period. The openness of the economy to imports stimulated competition and improved quality. Chinese consumer habits are now totally different from what they were: People are used to having television sets that work, they can wear western style clothes, eat better, and enjoy a better quality of life.

The macroeconomic policy of China has been pretty successful if you compare it with what happened in Russia and other economies in transition. The Chinese have major fiscal problems and since having liberalised the economy, government fiscal revenue has declined about from about a third of GDP in 1978 to about 11 % in 1995. They have been financing state enterprises by getting state banks to give loans to companies which were essentially bankrupt. So you have a weak financial structure and fiscal problems. Nevertheless, the rate of inflation in China has been on average about 10 or 11 % a year since 1978 whereas in Russia, from 1990 to 1994, the rate of inflation was nearly to 500% a year. The Chinese currency has depreciated 5 fold against the dollar since 1978 but the Russian rouble has deteriorated 8.5 thousand folds. The Chinese have been lucky in the sense that the basic credibility of the government has been much greater than in Russia. People have not been rushing away from the currency. They have also been in a situation where the monetarisation of the economy was increasing so there were seigniorage gains to the government which helped the situation.

5. FUTURE PROBLEMS

As far as the future is concerned, a major problem is state industrial enterprise. The average state enterprise employed 373 persons in 1995, and the number of enterprises has increased, from 84,000 in 1978 to 118,000 in 1995. It is politically difficult for the government to get rid of these enterprises because they have huge social security obligations. There is no social security for the rural population but industrial workers in state enterprises are provided with housing, education, health and even unemployment insurance, as the enterprises do not fire redundant workers. It will be a very delicate task to terminate these job-related privileges and create a better social security system. The task is all the more difficult as the government has serious fiscal problems, which have also weakened the creditworthiness of the state banking system.

Another major problem for China is inequality. Chinese regional inequality is now bigger than in any other country except Brazil. You also have a society where some people are getting very rich. The question is: how long will this be accepted without serious challenge to the legitimacy of the social order?

Finally, it is clear that the present growth rate will not continue forever. Some of the efficiency gains in the Reform period have had a once-for-all character. The rate of growth in agricultural productivity has slowed down. There is still a great potential for switching people out of agriculture into other sectors where productivity is higher, but rapid expansion of the urban population is considered to be politically risky.

CHAPTER 2
CHINESE ECONOMIC GROWTH: SOURCES AND PROSPECTS

WING THYE WOO [*]

1. INTRODUCTION

China's economic performance since economic reforms were initiated in late 1978 has been truly impressive.[1] GDP grew 9.3 percent annually in the 1979-93 period: per capita net income of farmers increased by 239 percent, and the per capita income of urban households increased by 152 percent.[2] The incidence of absolute poverty declined dramatically in the rural area, from 33 percent in 1978 to 12 percent in 1990. This achievement must count as one of the most successful poverty alleviation programs in the twentieth century.

This paper analyses the growth experience of China in the 1979-93 period with the objectives of, one, assessing the likelihood of attaining the 8 percent growth target, and, two, venturing an opinion on policy measures that could enhance stable growth without raising the fixed asset investment rate. The paper is organised as follows. Section 2 identifies the mechanics of aggregate growth. Section 3 takes a closer look at economic growth in the agricultural and industrial sector. Section 4 identifies the forces that generated the growth examined in the preceding two sections. Section 5 reviews the main challenges for economic growth in China, and concludes the paper with an assessment of future economic growth.

To anticipate the conclusions, the paper finds that the fixed asset investment rate of 32 percent in the Ninth five-year Plan would allow the achievement of the 8 percent growth target. There is in fact a high probability that the actual growth rate would exceed 8 percent if the Ninth five-year Plan

---

[*] Professor, Department of Economics, University of California, Davis.

1. See Sachs and Woo (1997) for a survey of the main competing interpretations of China's growth experience.

2. After the completion of this paper in October 1995, revised estimates of GDP and its components were released in the *1995 Statistical Yearbook of China* issued at the end of 1995. The old growth rates do not differ significantly from the revised growth rates. This paper uses the terminology that when the average growth rate for a period is given, the levels used in the calculation include the year before the period, e.g. the average 1979-93 GDP growth rate used the 1978 GDP level in its construction.

succeeds in establishing better market mechanisms and market institutions in more sectors of the economy, and hence raises the underlying rate of total factor productivity (TFP) growth.

2. THE SOURCES OF CHINESE ECONOMIC GROWTH

Measurement Issues

Before undertaking the growth accounting, it is necessary to confront two measurement issues that exaggerate the official GDP growth rates (see Table 2). The first issue is the estimation of GDP growth on a consistent set of base-year prices, and the second issue is the calculation of real value-added in the industry sector.[3]

The official GDP growth rates are calculated from different base years, e.g. 1980 prices for the 1981-90 period and 1990 prices for 1991 onward.[4] The conversion of the pre-1990 growth rates to 1990 basis will lower the growth rates in the earlier period because of the interaction between two developments. First, the ratio of agricultural price to industrial price was higher in 1990 than in 1980. Second, the industrial sector was the biggest contributor to economic growth in the 1985-1993 period. The negative movement in the agriculture-industry price ratio means that the growth of the industrial sector in the 1985-90 period will be smaller when measured in 1990 prices than in 1980 prices.

All real GDP (and their component) figures reported in this paper are based on 1990 prices. Columns (1) and (2) in Table 1 report, respectively, the official and consistent GDP growth rates. As expected, the re-calculation of GDP on a consistent set of base prices causes the average annual growth rate in the 1985-93 period to go from 9.7 percent to 9.4 percent.

The second mismeasurement is much more serious: the growth of the industry sector has been exaggerated in the official data. The construction of value-added in the industrial sector is, in broad strokes, done as follows. Every enterprise reports three series to the State Statistical Bureau (SSB): gross output value in current prices, gross output value in base-year prices, and value-added in current prices. The State Statistical Bureau then constructs an implicit price deflator from the first two series and uses it to deflate the third series to arrive at value-added in base-year prices.

---

3. More complete discussions of the problems with the Chinese statistical system are World Bank (1992) and (1994).

4. See page 54 of *Statistical Yearbook of China 1994*.

Table 1: GDP Growth Rate (in percent)

	Official	Consistently re-based on 1990 prices	Industrial output component re-deflated by factory-gate price index
	(1)	(2)	(3)
1978	11.7	10.9	-
1979	7.6	7.4	7.4
1980	7.8	6.9	7.3
1981	4.4	4.9	4.9
1982	8.3	8.6	8.3
1983	10.4	10.5	10.5
1984	14.6	14.5	14.9
1985	12.9	12	10.8
1986	8.5	8.2	8.8
1987	11.1	10.7	8.4
1988	11.2	10.5	8.5
1989	4.3	4.1	-0.2
1990	3.9	4.0	3.3
1991	8.0	8.0	7
1992	13.6	13.6	12.4
1993	13.4	13.4	8.9
Average 1979-93	9.3	9.2	8.1
Average 1979-84	8.9	8.8	8.9
Average 1985-93	9.7	9.4	7.5

Series (3) was also consistently based on 1990 prices.

One main drawback of the system is the reporting of gross output value in base-year prices. The State-Owned-Enterprises (SOEs), after long years of operation under the central planning system, are familiar with the correct calculation of this series. The Collective-Owned-Enterprises (COEs) that have flowered since 1984 are much less clear about how to do the computation, especially because the base-year (until 1990) was 1980 when most of them were not in existence. Since the Collective-Owned-Enterprises (COE's) are not supervised by the central ministries, they are under less pressure to report the real series accurately. So, many Collective-Owned-Enterprises (COEs) have reported identical figures for the gross output in current prices and gross output in base-year prices, either out of ignorance or out of convenience.

There is also the incentive problem about accurate reporting. The fact is that gross output in base-year prices has neither operational nor financial significance for the enterprises, it has significance only for their supervising bureaux. Since supervising bureaux like to report high growth performance to their head office, which can be interpreted as evidence of superior management ability, the enterprises have the incentive to oblige their supervisors. The result is that:

> "Many counties in China...overstate production figures so that they can be reclassified as towns, which benefit from added political and economic clout. And promotions for managers throughout much of the country's state-owned industry are based on output, not profit. When Jiangsu...persisted in reporting unusually high output numbers last year, [SSB's] auditors discovered that many poorer inland townships were systematically over-reporting production to keep up with booming townships along the coast."[5]

Another difficulty with the data on gross output in base-year prices is that the statistical system is flawed in its treatment of new products. It involves an estimate of what its base-year price would have been given its "quantity" attributes e.g. how many 286-chip is equivalent to one pentium chip in operational capacity. In response to the complications involved, a common practice by enterprises is to report the value of new products in current prices as the value in base-year prices. This over-statement of the real value of new products applies to statistical reports filed by both the SOEs and the COEs.

The by-product of all these tendencies to exaggerate the growth of real gross output is that the implicit deflators for the industrial output of SOEs and COEs consistently rose less than the factory-gate price index of industrial output, which is based on surveys of the prices (plan price and market price) received by a sample of industrial SOEs, mostly medium and large, for their products. (The term "factory gate price index" is the direct translation from the Chinese term, but the *Statistical Yearbook of China 1994* translates it as "Industrial Products Producer Price Index".

---

5. *The Asian Wall Street Journal Weekly*, January 30, 1995, "China's Politics, Inaccurate Methods Hinder Statistical Analysis of Economy."

Table 2 illustrates the difficulties of calculating real value-added in the industrial sector. Part A presents four price indices for industrial products from different sources, and Part B presents the rates of change of these price indices. Column (1) is an implicit deflator derived from the official GNP data, it is calculated from the nominal and real figures on value-added in the industry sector. Column (2) is also an implicit deflator and it is calculated from the official data on nominal and real *gross* industrial output. The close correspondence between column (1) and column (2) confirms the use of the latter in deflating nominal value-added.

Column (2) is the weighted average of two implicit deflators, the deflator for industrial SOE output and the deflator for industrial COE output, columns (3) and (4) respectively. Column (3) and (4) are constructed from the gross output value in current prices and gross output value in constant prices reported by industrial enterprises. Column (5) is the factory-gate price index.

The important thing to note is that the deflator for industrial COE output is unusually sluggish in the post-1984 period compared the deflator for industrial SOE output, the factory-gate price index of industrial output, and (not shown) the consumer price index.[6] In the 1990-93 period, the industrial COE output deflator rose 6 percent while the industrial SOE output deflator rose 35 percent, the factory-gate price index of industrial output rose 41 percent, and the consumer price index rose 26 percent. These figures support the widespread feeling that real value-added in the industrial COE sector is significantly exaggerated (especially, in the recent period) because of the reasons given earlier.

Part C of Table 2 shows the different levels of value-added in the industrial sector in 1990 prices obtained with the five price indices of Part A. Part D gives the growth rates of industry value-added. Real value added in 1993 is 5.1 times the 1978 level according to the official data, but is only 3.5 times when output is re-valued using factory-gate prices. This disparity is the result of the interaction between the greater exaggeration of real COE industrial output and the rapidly growing share of COEs in total industrial output.

---

6. The consumer price index is based on price surveys.

Table 2: Different Ways of Constructing Real Industrial Output

	Industry component of GDP accounts	Total gross industrial output	Industrial SOE gross output	Industrial collective gross output	Factory-gate price of industrial output
Part A: Deflators for Industrial Output According to Above Sources:					(1990=100)
1978	71.5	69.0	60.9	79.8	56.0
1979	72.4	70.1	62.4	78.1	56.8
1980	72.5	70.6	63.0	78.9	57.1
1981	73.2	70.9	63.4	63.4	57.2
1982	73	70.8	63.4	78.5	57.1
1983	73.1	70.8	63.5	78.4	57.1
1984	74.7	71.8	64.8	79.1	57.9
1985	78.2	75.4	68.7	82.1	62.9
1986	81.2	77.8	71.5	83.7	65.3
1987	83.7	81.6	76.1	86.6	70.4
1988	91.5	89.1	84.7	93.1	81.0
1989	97.7	99.2	97.3	100.5	96.1
1990	100.0	100.0	100.0	100.0	100.0
1991	103.7	102.9	105.4	99.9	106.2
1992	108.1	105.9	111.8	100.3	113.4
1993	122.8	118	134.8	105.8	140.6
Part B: Rate of Change in Price Index Calculated from above Sources:					
1979	1.3	1.5	2.6	-2.1	1.5
1980	0.2	0.7	0.9	1.0	0.5
1981	0.9	0.4	0.6	0.5	0.2
1982	-0.2	-0.1	0.1	-1.0	-0.2
1983	0.1	-0.0	0.2	-0.2	-0.1
1984	2.2	1.4	2.0	0.9	1.4
1985	4.6	5.0	6.0	3.8	8.7
1986	4.9	3.1	4.2	2.0	3.8
1987	2.1	4.8	6.3	3.4	7.9
1988	9.3	9.2	11.4	7.5	15.0
1989	6.8	11.3	14.8	8.0	18.6
1990	2.3	0.8	2.8	-0.5	4.1
1991	3.7	2.8	5.4	-0.1	6.2
1992	4.3	2.9	6.0	0.4	6.8
1993	13.5	11.0	20.6	5.4	24.0

Table 2: (cont.)

	Industry component of GDP accounts	Total gross industrial output	Industrial SOE gross output	Industrial collective gross output	Factory-gate price of industrial output
Part C: Total Real Industrial Output, (value added), after Deflation by Price Index from Above Source (in 1990 prices):					
1978	224.9	232.9	264.1	201.5	287.0
1979	244.5	252.6	283.5	226.6	311.4
1980	275.3	282.8	316.9	253.2	349.5
1981	280.0	288.9	323.3	258.4	357.9
1982	296.2	305.5	341	275.4	378.6
1983	325.0	335.7	374.1	303.2	416.3
1984	373.4	388.7	431.0	352.7	482.0
1985	441.3	457.3	502.4	420.2	548.4
1986	484.0	509.9	554.7	473.7	607.4
1987	547.9	562.2	603.0	529.5	651.1
1988	631.6	648.4	681.8	620.6	713.2
1989	663.5	653.8	666.5	645.1	674.9
1990	685.8	685.8	685.8	685.8	685.8
1991	780.3	786.1	767.4	809.2	761.5
1992	951.2	971.5	920.3	1025.1	906.8
1993	1151.9	1202.9	1049.3	1336.7	1005.3
Part D: Growth Rate of Industrial Value Added (in percent):					
1979	8.7	8.5	7.4	12.5	8.5
1980	12.6	12	11.8	11.7	12.3
1981	1.7	2.1	2.0	2.1	2.4
1982	5.8	5.8	5.5	6.6	5.8
1983	9.7	9.9	9.7	10.1	10
1984	14.9	15.8	15.2	16.4	15.8
1985	18.2	17.7	16.6	19.1	13.8
1986	9.7	11.5	10.4	12.7	11
1987	13.2	10.3	8.7	11.8	7.1
1988	15.3	15.3	13.1	17.2	9.6
1989	5.1	0.8	-2.2	4.0	-5.4
1990	3.4	4.9	2.9	6.3	1.6
1991	13.8	14.6	11.9	18	11.0
1992	21.9	23.6	19.9	26.7	19.1
1993	21.1	23.8	14.0	30.4	10.9

If the factory-gate price index were correct, then the official growth rate of the industrial sector in 1993 overstated the actual growth rate by 10 percentage points, see columns (1) and (5) in Part D of Table 2. Because the industrial sector was the biggest contributor to GDP growth, the re-valuation of real industrial output at factory-gate prices would lower the 1993 official GDP growth rate from 13.4 percent to 8.9 percent, see column (3) of Table 1. The sub-period GDP growth rates after the adjustments for base year changes and inadequate deflation of industrial output are:

GDP Growth Rates with Different Deflations of Industrial Output (in percent)

	1979-1984	1985-1993
Official data	8.9	9.7
Consistent base year (1990 prices)	8.8	9.4
Consistent base year (1990 prices) with re-valuation of industrial output using factory-gate price index	8.9	7.5

The important result from the re-valuation of industrial output is that there may not have been an acceleration in the 1985-93 average annual GDP growth rate from the 1979-84 average annual growth rate. Inadequate deflation of industrial output could have added as much as 1.9 percentage point[7] to the average growth rate of the 1985-93 period.

A word of caution is necessary at this point to set the correct way to interpret the results of this paper. This paper has not proved that the official measurement of non-SOE industrial output is incorrect because it has not proved that there was no change in the terms of trade between SOE industrial output and non-SOE industrial output. The industrial output of SOEs and non-SOEs may be sufficiently non-overlapping and non-substitutable that the more rapid growth of the latter has caused the terms of trade to move against non-SOE industrial output. Furthermore, the paper has not proved that the factory-gate price index is the correct price index to use.

Given the data problems identified above necessary, point estimates of average GDP growth and average Total Factor Productivity (TFP) growth are less useful than the respective plausible ranges within which the true means lie. Thus, this paper will calculate point estimates and the plausible ranges of these point estimates. In short, this paper acknowledges the data measurement problems that are well known and recognised by the State Statistical Bureau of China, and attempts to estimate the magnitudes of these data problems.

---

7. This number is different from the implied number of the preceding figures because of rounding errors.

The correct way, therefore, to look at the preceding GDP growth rates (and the subsequent estimates of TFP growth rates) is to regard them as the *upper and lower ends of the respective plausible ranges* within which the actual GDP (and TFP) growth rates lie. The upper end of the estimates on GDP growth is given by the official data (re-calculated on a consistent base year) and the lower end of the estimates is calculated by re-valuing industry output with the factory-gate price index.

One important issue that needs to be clarified here is the possibility of a relationship between the estimated GDP level and the estimated GDP growth rate. As is well known, the actual level of GDP may be understated by official data. The point that must be understood is that the understatement of the level *does not automatically mean* that the official growth rate is also understated. Unless it can be shown that the unmeasured part of GDP has been growing consistently faster than the measured part, one could not conclude that the official growth rate is an understatement. One could in fact argue the opposite: the existence of unmeasured economic activities means that an improving statistical reporting system would begin to count them, treating the existing activities as new activities, and hence exaggerate the growth rate. So an understated level of GDP is likely to produce an overstated rate of GDP growth as data reporting improves over time.

Given the various factors that bias the estimate of GDP growth rate in opposing directions, it is important to bear in mind that the aim of this paper is to provide respective plausible ranges for the average GDP and TFP growth rates and not just point estimates of them. The terms of trade might had indeed turned against COEs' industrial products, such that the use of the factory-gate price index would understate the quantity of industrial output produced. But the improvements in China's data collection could exaggerate output growth by counting existing activities as new activities.

The Delineation of Growth Phases

China's economic growth can be divided into two analytical phases by their sources of growth. The first phase is the 1979-84 period where the agricultural sector was an important contributor to growth. Comprehensive liberalisation of the primary sector was initiated at the end of 1978 by expanding the use of agricultural markets, and decollectivising agriculture. Some production incentives (notably, profit-retention and bonus) were introduced for some classes of secondary and tertiary activities during the first phase of reform. The average annual growth rate for the 1979-84 period was 8.8 percent. Agriculture and industry made almost equal contribution to the output expansion, 32 percentage points and 34 percentage points respectively, see Part 1 of Table 3.

The impressive growth of the first phase led to broader liberalisation of the secondary and tertiary sectors in mi-1984. The most radical liberalisation occurred in the rural areas with the lifting of restrictions on the formation of community-owned production units, the TVEs.[8]   The SOEs, located mainly in urban areas, were liberalised by devolving to them some decision-making power from the supervising industrial bureaux.

The average annual growth rate in second phase, 1985-93, was 9.4 percent. Industry accounted for 57.5 percent of the increase in output; and the tertiary sector greatly out-stripped the primary sector in terms of contribution, 25 percent versus 12 percent. The biggest contributor to GDP growth is the industrial COE sector, 29 percentage points.   Industrial individual-owned enterprises accounted for 8 percentage points of the aggregate output growth.

It is important to stress however that the conventional view regarding the sources of growth in the 1985-93 period remains unchanged after re-valuing industrial output with factory-gate prices, see Part 2 of Table 3. Industry now accounted for 47 percent of the output expansion, the tertiary sector for 31 percent and the primary sector for 14 percent. The industrial sector remained the chief engine of growth, and the non-state sector was in the driver seat.

The leading role of the industry sector in GDP growth since 1978 (even more so since 1984) places China's economic growth within the context of traditional economic development. The unusually large contribution of the tertiary sector to China's growth places China's experience within the context of economic transition from traditional central planning. Central planning has traditionally regarded service activities as "unproductive",[9] and hence has suppressed them. The rapid development of the service sector after 1978 reflects its relative underdevelopment because of its prior suppression.

---

8. Given that the unleashing of the rural TVEs brought great dynamism to the economy, it is hence not right to characterize phase two, as some have done, as reforms of the urban sector.

9. Most service activities are not counted in Net Material Product, the aggregate income measure used in socialist economies.

Table 3: Share of contribution to GDP growth rate by sector (and by ownership in the industry sector) (in percentage points, each row sums to 100)

Part 1: Using Official Data, with series consistently re-based on 1990 prices

Sectoral contribution	Primary sector	Industrial sector				Construction sector	Tertiary sector
		State-owned (soe)	Collective-owned (coe)	Individual-owned	Other forms		
Growth in 79-93	16.5	13.8	25.0	5.9	6.9	5.7	26.1
Growth in 79-84	31.78	20.3	12.8	0.2	0.8	5.2	28.9
Growth in 85-93	11.6	11.7	28.9	7.8	8.9	5.9	25.3

Part 2: After re-deflating industrial output by factory-gate price index

Sectoral contribution	Primary sector	Industrial sector				Construction sector	Tertiary sector
		State-owned (soe)	Collective-owned (coe)	Individual-owned	Other forms		
Growth in 79-93	18.7	12.9	20.3	5.34	6.4	6.5	29.8
Growth in 79-84	29.3	21.8	16.2	0.2	1.0	4.8	26.6
Growth in 85-93	14.3	9.1	22.0	7.6	8.8	7.2	31.1

The Mechanics of Growth

The growth accounting exercise is based on the three sectors - primary, secondary (industry and construction) and tertiary - as defined by Chinese statistics. Each sector is assumed to be characterised by a Cobb-Douglas production function, and the result is:

$$Y = j(a_i x_i^{\beta i} z_i^{(1-\beta i)}) L^{\beta i} K^{(1-\beta i)}$$

Where:

Y	= GDP
L	= total labor force
K	= total capital stock
w_i	= sector i's share of GDP
x_i	= sector i's share of labor force
z_i	= sector i's share of capital stock

sector 1 = primary sector (agriculture, forestry and fishing),

sector 2 = secondary sector (industry and construction)

sector 3 = tertiary sector.

GDP growth can be decomposed into portions that are due to capital accumulation, labor force growth, and total factor productivity (TFP) growth:

$$(dY/Y) = (dL/L)\beta w_i \beta_i + (dK/K)\beta w_i(1-\beta_i) + \beta w_i \beta_i(dx_i/x_i)$$
$$+ \beta w_i(d\beta_i/\beta_i) + \beta w_i(1-\beta_i)(dz_i/z_i)$$

where: TFP Growth = $\beta w_i \beta_i(dx_i/x_i) + \beta w_i(d\beta_i/\beta_i) + \beta w_i(1-\beta_i)(dz_i/z_i)$

TFP growth is in turn partitioned into, what we call here, labor reallocation effect and net TFP growth:

labor reallocation effect = $\beta w_i \beta_i(dx_i/x_i)$

net TFP growth   = $\beta w_i(d\beta_i/\beta_i) + \beta w_i(1-\beta_i)(dz_i/z_i)$

Net TFP growth is the residual that contains technological improvements.

Labor reallocation is singled out for attention because the bulk of the Chinese labor force is peasant farmers, a third of whom lived below the absolute poverty line in 1978. Sachs and Woo (1994) have argued that this "surplus labor" feature[10] has made China's transition from centrally planning

---

10. Agence France Press (December 7, 1993) reported the Agriculture Minister Liu Jiang as saying that there were 150 million excess farm workers (out of a rural labor force of 450 million).

fundamentally different from the transition of Central and Eastern Europe and the former Soviet Union (CEEFSU). Specifically, they argued that the marketization of a centrally planned economy means normal economic development for China but structural adjustment for a CEEFSU country. The intersectoral shift of labor (away from agriculture) increases aggregate output when the marginal product of labor (MPL) in the primary sector is lower than the respective MPLs in the secondary and service sectors. Chow (1993) found the marginal value product of labor in 1978 to be 63 yuan in agriculture, 1027 yuan in industry, 452 yuan in construction, 739 yuan in transportation and 1809 yuan in commerce.[11]

There could have been further refinements to the preceding decomposition formula but the absence of data prevented them. Net TFP could have been decomposed further; for example, to get the contribution from the intersectoral shift of capital, and the contribution from change in ownership structure. But both of these contributions would require making bold assumptions; the first would require knowledge about the sectoral distribution of capital, and the second would require knowledge on the distribution of capital and labor by ownership in each sector.

Given the unreliability of data on the sectoral distribution of capital stock, upon which estimates of sectoral β's would have to be based, we drew upon the production function literature on China to generate a range of TFP growth rates by using different values for different values of a common β; specifically, β =0.4, 0.5, and 0.6. I rely on Li Jing Wen's (1992) estimates of the capital stock for the growth accounting. I use compound rates of growth instead of the arithmetic average growth rates in the analysis.[12]

The growth accounting exercise is conducted for the entire 1979-1993 period and for two subperiods, 1979-84 and 1985-93. The delineation of the subperiods correspond, one, to the policy regime change toward accelerating reforms in the nonagriculture sectors, and, two, to the emergence of industry as the undisputed primary engine of growth. The growth performance of the 1985-93 subperiod may be a better guide (than that of the entire period) to understanding the future growth prospects of China. This is because future Chinese growth is likely to be led by the industrial sectors as in the 1985-93 period.

Table 4 reports the contribution of each factor to growth. A range of estimates for each contribution was generated by the two ways of constructing real industrial output (official method and factory-gate prices method) and the three values of β (0.4, 0.5 and 0.6). China's high investment rate and low initial capital stock caused the capital stock to grow 9.8 percent annually in the

11. Figures are expressed in 1952 output values.

12. The difference between them is minuscule e.g. the compound growth rates of GDP are slightly lower than the simple arithmetic average growth rates by about 0.05 percentage point.

1979-93 period.   Capital accumulation was responsible for 3.9 to 5.9 percentage points of the GDP growth rate; and labor force expansion was responsible for 1.1 to 1.6 percentage points. This meant that TFP growth contributed 1.1 to 3.6 percentage points to the 1979-93 GDP growth rate.

The 1985-93 subperiod in Table 4 is interesting in that during the period when industry was the major source of growth, capital accumulation accelerated to raise its growth contribution to the 4.4 - 6.6 percentage point range from the 3.2 - 4.9 percentage point range of the 1979-84 subperiod. The slowdown of TFP growth is real, it is not the result of data adjustment or of different values, e.g. TFP growth calculated from official GDP data dropped from 3.2 percent to 2.6 percent when $\beta = 0.5$. The biggest drop in TFP growth occurred in the case of industrial output deflated by factory-gate prices and $\beta = 0.4$, from 2.8 percent in 1979-84 to -01 percent in 1985-93.

Table 5 decomposes TFP growth into the labor re-allocation effect and net TFP growth. It should be noted that the official data on sectoral distribution of labor should be used critically. The official estimate of labor in agriculture is based on registered residency status, it is an overstatement because of illegal rural migration, especially to coastal Township and Village Enterprises (TVEs). The official estimate of the size of illegal migration is 80 million and the World Bank's highest estimate is 150 million. The official estimate (80 million) does not include the 20 million people who migrate within their home districts.[13]   In light of this data problem, two sets of estimates for labor reallocation effect and net TFP growth are conducted. The first set reported in Part A of Table 5 gives the minimum value of the labor reallocation effect by using the official figures on the sectoral distribution of labor. The second set reported in Part B of Table 5 assumes illegal rural migration to be 100 million since 1984, with 60 percent of the migrants ending up in industrial jobs.[14]

Part A of Table 5 reports that labor reallocation added only 0.5 to 0.7 percentage point to the 1979-93 growth rate. Furthermore, it shows that the labor reallocation effect is weaker in the 1985-93 subperiod. This smaller labor reallocation effect is contrary to the evident increasing outflow of agriculture labor after 1984 with the steady liberalisation of regulations governing TVE establishment and activities e.g. TVEs being free to participate directly in international trade from 1987 onward. This contradiction suggests that the official data on sectoral labor distribution must be adjusted to reflect the illegal migration that has occurred, i.e. at least making use of the official estimates of the size of the "floating population."

---

13. *Far Eastern Economic Review*, "Irresistible Force," April 4, 1996.

14. The sum of the official estimate of 80 million who moved out of home district and the 20 million who moved within their home districts.

The important finding in Part A of Table 5 is that the previous finding in Table 4 of the fall in TFP in the 1985-93 subperiod *cannot* be explained by the diminishing of the labor reallocation effect. Net TFP fell in the 1985-93 subperiod when official GDP data and official sectoral labor distribution data are used, regardless of the value of β. In short, the finding of a decline in technological improvements in the second subperiod is a robust one.

Part B of Table 5 reports that the labor reallocation effect increased the GDP growth rate by 0.9 to 1.3 percentage point in the 1979-93 period, and by 1.0 to 1.6 percentage point in the 1985-93 subperiod. The result is that net TFP growth is 0.2 to 2.3 percent for the entire period, and -1.1 to 1.9 percent for the second subperiod.

I draw three conclusions from Tables 4 and 5. The first conclusion is that the appearance of three cases of negative net TFP growth in the 1985-93 subperiod suggests that the use of the factory-gate price index may have understated the real amount of industrial output. The explosive growth of TVE output is likely to have worsened its terms of trade *vis-à-vis* SOE output. It is possible that 1985-93 GDP growth may be understated by as little as 0.9 to 1.2 percentage point instead of the 1.9 percentage point suggested by the use of factory-gate prices.[15] The second conclusion comes from the robust finding of lower net TFP growth in the second subperiod. The slowdown reflected the fact that a part of the TFP growth unleashed by the 1978 reforms was a *one-time recovery in efficiency* from the decade-long Cultural Revolution and from the over-regulation of the economy be central-planning. The agricultural reforms may have accounted for a large part of the initial high net TFP growth.

---

15. Net TFP growth would thus range from -0.3 to 1.2 percentage points in the 1985-93 period.

Table 4: Contributions of Capital Accumulation, Labor Force Growth and Total Factor Productivity (TFP) Growth to GDP Growth Rate

(a) Compound growth rate of GDP, using official 1978-93 data that have been consistently re-based on 1990 prices (in percent)			
Average 1979-93	9.1		
Average 1979-84	8.8		
Average 1985-93	9.3		
(b) Compound growth rate of GDP, using official 1978-93 data that have been consistently re-based on 1990 prices (in percent)			
Average 1979-93	8.0		
Average 1979-84	8.9		
Average 1985-93	7.5		
	Compound growth rate (percent)	Contributions to growth rate		
		Beta = 0.40 0.50 0.60 (percentage points)		
(c) Contribution of capital accumulation to GDP growth			
Average 1979-93	9.8	5.9	4.9	3.9
Average 1979-84	8.1	4.9	4.1	3.2
Average 1985-93	11.0	6.6	5.5	4.4
(d) Contribution of labor force expansion to GDP growth			
Average 1979-93	2.7	1.1	1.4	1.6
Average 1979-84	3.1	1.2	1.6	1.9
Average 1985-93	2.5	1.0	1.3	1.5
(e) Contribution of TFP growth to GDP growth (with official industrial value added data)			
Average 1979-93		2.1	2.8	3.6
Average 1979-84		2.7	3.2	3.7
Average 1985-93		1.8	2.6	3.5
(f) Contribution of TFP growth to GDP growth (with industrial value added re-deflated by factory-gate price index)			
Average 1979-93		1.1	1.8	2.5
Average 1979-84		2.8	3.3	3.8
Average 1985-93		-0.1	0.7	1.6

Beta = the exponent of labor in the Cobb-Douglas production function.
Compound growth rate for 1979-93 is calculated using 1978 and 1993 level.

The second conclusion comes from the robust finding of lower net TFP growth in the second subperiod. The slowdown reflected the fact that a part of the TFP growth unleashed by the 1978 reforms was a *one-time recovery in efficiency* from the decade-long Cultural Revolution and from the over-regulation of the economy be central-planning. The agricultural reforms may have accounted for a large part of the initial high net TFP growth.

The third conclusion is that when illegal immigration is taken into account, the reallocation of labor from agriculture accounted for 37 to 54 percent of TFP growth in the whole period, and 45 to 100 percent of TFP growth in the second subperiod. To appreciate how large this effect is, I note that labor reallocation from the farm sector accounted for only 13 percent of TFP growth in the United States in the 1948-69 period.[16] The large labor allocation effect in China reflects the existence of large amount of labor employed in low-productivity agriculture and the success of the post-1978 Chinese reforms in creating higher-productivity jobs in the industry and service sectors.

To summarize the range of estimates, the official growth rates could be reasonably decomposed to:

(in percentage points per annum)	1979-1993	1985-1993
Official growth rate	9.3	9.7
Inconsistent use of base years	0.2	0.3
Overstatement of industrial output	0.5 to 0.7	0.9 to 1.2
Capital accumulation	4.9	5.5
Labor force growth	1.3	1.1
Reallocation of labor from agriculture	1.1	1.3
Net TFP growth	1.1 to 1.3	0.3 to 0.6

16. Denison (1974, pp.127) reported that U.S. national income grew 3.85 percent annually in the 1948-69 period, TFP growth was 1.75 percent, and labor reallocation from the farm sector added 0.23 percentage points to overall growth.

Table 5: Decomposing Total Factor Productivity (TFP) Growth into Labor Reallocation Effect and Net TFP Growth.

	TFP growth rate from using official industrial value added data			TPF growth rate from using industrial value added re-deflated by factory-gate price-index		
Beta =	0.40	0.50	0.60	0.40	0.50	0.60
Section A: Decomposition TFP growth rate without considering illegal migration						
Labor Reallocation Effect (in percentage points)						
Avg 79-93	0.5	0.6	0.7	0.5	0.6	0.7
Avg 79-84	0.6	0.7	0.9	0.6	0.8	0.9
Avg 85-93	0.4	0.5	0.6	0.4	0.5	0.6
Net TFP Growth (in percentage points)						
Avg 79-93	1.7	2.2	2.8	0.6	1.1	1.7
Avg 79-84	2.1	2.5	2.8	2.2	2.15	2.9
Avg 85-93	1.4	2.1	2.9	-0.5	0.3	1.0
Section B: Decomposition TFP growth rate assuming illegal migration to be 100 million from 1984 to 1993						
Labor Reallocation Effect (in percentage points)						
Avg 79-93	0.9	1.1	1.3	0.9	1.1	1.3
Avg 79-84	0.6	0.7	0.9	0.6	0.8	0.9
Avg 85-93	1.0	1.3	1.6	1.1	1.4	1.6
Net TFP Growth (in percentage points)						
Avg 79-93	1.3	1.8	2.3	0.2	0.7	1.1
Avg 79-84	2.1	2.5	2.8	2.2	2.5	2.9
Avg 85-93	0.7	1.3	1.9	-1.2	-0.6	-0.4

Beta = exponent of labor variable in Cobb-Douglas production function.
Average output share during the period was used in the calculations.

I must emphasize that the above point estimates of TFP growth, labor allocation effect and net TFP growth should be considered together with the range of estimates in Table 5. It is therefore re-assuring that two recent examinations of China's growth performance have arrived at estimates almost similar to those above. For the 1979-90 period, Borensztein and Ostry (1996) have calculated the labor reallocation effect to be about 1.0 percentage point and the plausible range of TFP growth to be -1.0 to 3.8 percent. World Bank (1996) decomposed the 10.2 percent GDP growth of the 1985-94 period into 6.6 percentage points from factor accumulation, 1.1 percentage point from labor reallocation effect and 2.5 percentage points from net TFP growth.[17] While the World Bank study did not address the issue about the overstatement of industrial output caused by underdeflation when it presented the preceding figures in its main report, it acknowledged this problem (by citing the October 1995 draft of this paper) in a technical annex and noted that its "correction lowers overall efficiency growth by about 1%".[18]

Hu and Khan (1996) decomposed the growth of Chinese-defined National Income (which is close to Net Material Product, the output concept of command economies) and found annual TFP growth to be 3.9 percent during 1979-94. This high TFP growth was generated by ignoring the issue of underdeflation of nominal output and by using a new capital stock series that they constructed. The Hu and Khan capital stock grew 7 percent annually compared to the over 10 percent annual growth in the capital stock constructed by Li (1992) and Nehru and Dhareshawar (1993).[19]

I now turn for a closer look at the agricultural, industrial and foreign sectors to see if they support our future TFP scenario.

4. THE SECTORAL GROWTH SITUATION

The Agriculture Sector

Economic growth came with a rush to the countryside after 1978 with the dismantling of the commune system, the raising of the purchase prices for grain, and the legalization of free markets for many agriculture products. Rural income jumped 17.6 percent in 1979, and income growth stayed at the two-digit level until 1985, see Table 6. The dynamic growth of rural income

---

17. I have converted the terminology of Table A in World Bank (1996, Volume I, pp. 12) into the terminology used in this paper, e.g. its definition of TFP growth deviated from the standard usage of Denison (1969) by listing reallocation of agricultural labor as distinct from TFP growth.

18. Footnote 7 in Annex 4 of Volume 2 (pp. 32) of World Bank (1996).

19. This study and Borensztein and Ostry (1996) are based on Li's (1992) capital stock data, and World Bank (1996) is based on Nehru and Dhareshawar's (1993) capital stock data; with updating in all cases for recent years

ended in 1985 when income grew only 4 percent. The average annual rural income growth rate was 2.6 percent in the 1985-94 period compared to the average growth rate of 15 percent in the 1979-84 period.

The course of rural income growth is largely the result of the sharp rise in grain yield in the 1979-84 period and the stagnation in grain yield from 1985 onward, see Table 7. The evidence suggests that yield growth was artificially suppressed in the pre-1978 period by the chaos of the Cultural Revolution that lasted from 1966 to 1977. When economic liberalization of the agriculture sector occurred at the end of 1978, there was a one-time gain in production efficiency, raising the growth in grain yield to 5.7 percent from the 3.1 percent of the preceding twelve years. The drop in grain yield after 1984 was across the board; rice yield growth dropped from 5.1 percent to 1.3 percent from 1985 onward, and wheat yield growth dropped from 8 percent to 2 percent.

The troubling aspect is that yield growth in the 1985-94 period is lower than in the 1966-77 period. One reason why yield growth is lower now may lie in the reduced amount of rural infrastructure investment since 1979. Real public capital construction is lower in 1994 than in 1978, and this has been true for every year since 1980, see Table 6.

The Industrial Sector

The single consensus from the many studies on TFP growth in the industrial sector is that TFP growth in the industrial COEs was positive and greatly exceeded that in the industrial SOEs; e.g. Huang and Meng (1995), Jefferson, Rawski and Zheng (1992), and Woo, Hai, Jin and Fan (1994) who will be designated HM, JRZ and WHJF respectively.[20] For example, JRZ estimated the annual TFP growth rate in the 1980-88 period to be 2.4 percent for SOEs and 4.6 percent for COEs.

The issue under contention is whether the SOEs has had positive TFP growth. Using survey samples, HM and WHJF found the TFP growth rate for SOEs to be, respectively, -4.7 percent in the 1986-90 period, and zero in the 1985-88 period. When WHJF deflated their intermediate inputs in the same way as JRZ, they found the same result as JRZ, 2.4 percent for TFP growth. However, WHJF found that the JRZ deflation method caused the implicit deflator for the value-added (VAD, value-added deflator) of SOEs in their sample to decline secularly throughout the sample period when CPI was rising steadily. Upon examination, the VAD in JRZ and those in Groves, Hong, McMillan and Naughton (GHMN, 1994

---

20. However, given the evidence in the preceding sections that COE output is likely to have been overstated, even this conclusion is tentative.

Table 6 : Rural Income, Grain Yield, Stated Capital Investment in Agriculture, and Urban-Rural Income Ratio

	Growth rate of rural per capital real income (percent)	Growth rate of yield (percent)		Goverment expenditure for capital construction in agriculture sector (in 1978 prices)	Urban-rural income ratio
		grain	rice	mill yuan	
1978	NA	NA	NA	5114	NA
1979	17.6	11.8	6.8	6149	NA
1980	14.4	-3.2	-2.5	4763	NA
1981	14.3	3.3	4.4	2363	2.2
1982	18.9	10.6	13.2	2824	1.9
1983	13.3	8.6	4.3	3361	1.8
1984	11.4	6.2	5.3	3255	1.8
1985	4.0	-3.7	-2.2	3359	1.7
1986	0.5	1.3	1.7	3763	2.0
1987	2.8	2.6	1.4	3721	2.0
1988	0.3	-0.8	-2.5	2742	1.9
1989	-7.5	1.3	4.3	2951	2.1
1990	9.5	8.3	4.0	3735	2.0
1991	0.6	-1.5	-1.5	3980	2.2
1992	5.7	3.3	2.9	4196	2.2
1993	3.4	3.2	0.9	3782	2.4
1994	7.4	-1.6	-0.4	3564	2.4

Real rural and urban income obtained by using real and urban CPI
respectively. Real capital construction obtained by industrial products producer
price index.

Table 7: Rice, Wheat and Grain Yield

Trend Growth of Grain Yield (per percent)			
Period	Grain	Rice	Wheat
1966-1977	3.1	1.4	4.4
1978-1984	5.7	5.1	8.0
1985-1994	2.0	1.3	1.9

and 1995), two studies that also found large positive TFP growth in the 1980-89, also declined secularly over their sample periods.[21]   Such opposite trends between the CPI and the VAD created by JRZ's and GHMN's deflation methods is troubling because such occurrences are internationally unprecedented.

Naughton (1994) and JRZ (1994) have argued that a declining VAD is to be expected when input prices rise more than output prices.   However, their arguement is not correct because a relative rise in input prices is only a necessary condition but not a sufficient one.   The condition for a secularly declining VAD is given by:

$$[(P_t^G-P_0^G)/P_0^G] < [1+(a_t-a_0)/a_0]*[P_0^I M_0/P_0^G Q_0]*[(P_t^I-P_0^I)/P_0^I]$$

where:

M_i = intermediate inputs in period i in physical units;

Q_i = gross output in period i in physical units;

P_i^G = price of gross output in period i;

P_i^I = price of intermediate input in period i;

$a_i = M_i/Q_i$, the input-output coefficient in period i.[22]

We should note that the quadrupling and doubling of oil prices in 1973 and 1978 respectively did not cause any country's GDP deflator to decline.   A declining VAD is also unlikely to be the product of gradual reforms because neither Polish nor Hungarian industrial VAD declined for sustained periods during their pre-1989 gradual reforms.   WHJF attributed JRZ's and GHMN's declining VADs to their output price deflators being under-stated and their intermediate input price deflators being over-stated.

In a recent article, JRZ (1996) defended their deflators for gross output and intermediate inputs, and attributed the declining VAD to the *unusual production structure* of China's manufacturing sector: China's manufacturing sector had an usually low gross value added (GVA) to gross output value (GOV) ratio, i.e.

---

21 The declining VAD in GHMN cannot be discerned in the two articles themselves, this facet was revealed in Naughton (1994) for GHMN (1995). I assume it to be also true for GHMN (1994) because it uses the same deflation techniques and sample as GHMN (1995).

22. The legacy of central planning is that at the beginning of industrial reform, prices of intermediate inputs to industry were artificially suppressed and prices of industrial goods artificially raised in order to concentrate revenue in the industrial sector to make revenue collection convenient for the state. So we expect $(P_0^I M_0/P_t^I M_t)$ to be much smaller than unity. As the prices of intermediate inputs have risen relative to output prices, the economizing by enterprises on the use of intermediate inputs renders $[1-(a_t-a_0)/a_0]$ less than unity. The net result is that intermediate input prices have to rise significantly more than output prices in order for a declining VAD to occur.

manufacturing sector had an usually low gross value added (GVA) to gross output value (GOV) ratio, i.e.

$$(P_t^I M_t / P_t^G Q_t)_{China} > (P_t^I M_t / P_t^G Q_t)_{USA}$$

They computed the (GVA/GOV) ratio to be 46% for the United States, 40% for Japan, 45% for West Germany and 44% for the United Kingdom compared to the (GVA/GOV) ratio for China which was 33% in 1980, 31% in 1984, 29% in 1988, and 25% in 1992.

However, JRZ's finding of an unusual Chinese industrial structure for China appears to be a fragile one. Specifically, JRZ's proposition which is based on Industrial Yearbook data does not hold when the 1987 Input-Output Table data are used instead. *The Industrial Yearbook* data are based on the financial reports (similar to information given to the industrial census) filed by the enterprises, while the Input-Output Table data adjusted the industrial census data to be compatible with economy-wide input-output flows. Ren Ruoen (private communications) rendered the GVA data from China's Input-Output Table to be consistent with the US Industrial Census definition of GVA by adding in payments to intermediate services[23] The results of Ren Ruoen's calculations is that the ratio of gross value added to gross output value for the industrial sector was 42% for China when Input-Output Table data were used. Our calculations, using US Commerce Department data, found the ratio to be 44 percent for the USA. Each of China's industrial sectoral (GVA/GOV) from the Input-Output Table was not only larger than the (GVA/GOV) from the *Industrial Yearbook*, but also closer to the US sectoral (GVA/GOV).

Finally, JRZ's finding of low and secularly declining (GVA/GOV) ratio for China suggest to us under-measurement of GVA caused by the growing appropriation of capital income by SOE personnel. Fan and Woo (1996) have shown that one unintended result of granting increasing operational autonomy to the SOE managers is that they have over time learned how to use various accounting subterfuges to overstate production costs in order to transfer enterprise income to themselves and the workers. This is why (GVA/GOV) calculated from the financial information supplied by the enterprises has been declining steadily in the reform period, and why the adjustment of GVA to be compatible with economy-wide flows produced much higher (GVA/GOV). This also explains why China's SOEs have been running greater losses every year, even in years of high growth and in sectors where entry by non-state enterprises has been minimal.

---

23. The GVA data reported in the *Industrial Yearbook* are supposed to already include payments to intermediate services; see Ren (forthcoming).

A One-Time Improvement in Industrial Efficiency

In light of the earlier analysis on grain yield, I suspect that the ending of the economic incoherence generated by the Cultural Revolution caused a one-time catch-up in the efficiency of SOEs during the 1979-84 period. After that initial rebound, the incremental decentralization measures introduced since 1984 have failed to induce the industrial SOEs to improve their efficiency on a sustained basis.

My hypothesis would reconcile the findings of positive TFP growth in SOEs in the pre-1985 period[24] with the findings of zero TFP growth in the post-1984 period. This hypothesis implies that a study that finds positive TFP growth in industrial SOEs in the post-1978 period would find zero TFP growth after dropping the 1979-84 period from the estimation. This hypothesis is tested in Table 8 using the data on industrial SOEs and industrial TVEs in Wu and Wu (1994).

Part A of Table 8 treats the data as in Wu and Wu (1994), output and capital were deflated using the implicit industry deflator from the GDP accounts. Part A shows that TFP growth rates in SOEs ranged from 0.9 percent to 1.9 percent over the 1979-91 period. However, the SOEs' TFP growth rate went to zero in two of the three cases when the estimation period was restricted to 1985-91. The TFP growth rate in TVEs was significantly positive in the subperiod as well in the entire period, but usually lower in the former. Part A supports the hypothesis that there was a strong one-time productivity gain when decentralization reforms were first introduced.

However, there are two measurement issues with the data used in Part A. First, Wu and Wu's method of constructing the capital stock biases the estimation to produce a positive TFP result. This is because the capital stock of any period was obtained by deflating that period's nominal net fixed assets (which is original book value minus depreciation) of each period by the industrial VAD from the national accounts. This continuous deflation of the remaining capital stock in subsequent periods steadily reduced the measured size of the remaining capital stock, hence boosting up estimates of TFP growth. Second, from the earlier discussion, the industrial VAD from the national accounts understates the actual inflation. This exaggeration of real output growth could mean exaggeration of TFP growth.

Part B of Table 8 re-estimates the TFP growth rates after adjusting Wu and Wu's data. The official depreciation rates were applied to the nominal fixed assets data to derive the nominal investment in each period. After deflating the investment flow with the factory-gate price index, the real capital stock was constructed using the perpetual inventory method under the

---

24. Chen, Wang, Zheng, Jefferson and Rawski (1988), Dollar (1990), Granick (1990) and Jefferson (1990).

assumption of a 5 percent depreciation rate. Output was also deflated by the factory-gate price index.

I attribute the better performance of the TVEs to them being fundamentally different from SOEs in three important ways. The first difference is that TVEs face less of a principal-agent problem than the SOEs because of shorter supervision distance. The direct linkage in TVEs between local people's working efforts and their economic benefits not only reduces the cost of supervision but also improves the local owners' incentives to monitor the management, and exert pressures on managers to improve the business.

The second difference is that TVEs face hard budget constraints. Being a non-state enterprise means that the rescue of a bankrupt TVE is not the state's responsibility. In the last economic downtown, the number of industrial TVEs fell from 7.7 million in 1988 to 7.2 million in 1990 while the number of industrial SOEs increased from 99 thousand to 104 thousand.

The third difference is that TVEs can implement institutional innovations without the approval of the central government. The most recent locally-initiated institutional development is the transformation of the TVEs into "share-holding co-operatives." The TVEs are equitised and a portion of the shares are given to the *original* residents. This freedom of TVEs has enabled them to move closer to best international practices in corporate governance.

The Foreign-Funded and International Trade Sectors

The direct contribution of foreign-funded enterprises (FFE) to GDP growth has been small. As industrial FFEs account for less than 9 percentage points of output growth in 1985-93, their effect on economy-wide TFP is small even if there is significant direct TFP growth in FFE production. FFEs' contribution to economy-wide TFP is increased to the extent that competition with FFEs and emulation of FFEs' management practices by domestic firms increase their efficiency. This externality is likely to be small.

The international trade sector has increased from 10 percent of GNP in 1978 to 36 percent in 1993. This unusually high trade/GDP ratio reflected the tremendous explosion of processing and assembly operations attracted by cheap Chinese labor. The international trade sector has created positive TFP growth by moving labor from low-productivity agriculture to higher-productivity industrial production. Given the large pool of low-cost unskilled rural labor, the positive TFP rate from labor re-allocation is sustainable in the medium run. The opening up to international trade also allowed comparative advantage to increase allocative efficiency through changes in the composition of output. The increasing direct competition from imports has exerted pressure on domestic producers to improve their operations, and this pressure will grow as President Jiang Zemin's pledge at the 1995 APEC meeting to reduce China's tariffs is implemented.

Numbers without brackets are TFP growth expressed in percent per annum : Numbers within brackets are absolute values of the t-statistics		
Beta=0.4	Beta=0.5	Beta=0.6
Part A: Wu and Wu (1994) data State-Owned Enterprises		
1978-91	0.9 (3.4)	1.4 (6.0)	1.9 (8.3)
1984-91	-0.2 (0.5)	0.5 (1.0)	1.0 (-2.4)
Rural Enterprises (township-village-private owned)		
1978-91	3.5 (10.1)	4.2 (14.0)	5.0 (16.9)
1984-91	2.6 (2.8)	4.1 (4.4)	5.5 (6.2)
Part B : Used alternative Measures of Capital Stock and Output State-Owned Enterprises		
1978-91	-1.8 (3.3)	-1.1 (2.2)	-0.5 (1.0)
1984-91	-5.2 (10.0)	-4.4 (8.3)	-3.6 (-6.7)
Rural Enterprises (township-village-private owned)		
1978-91	1.2 (2.0)	2.0 (3.8)	2.8 (6.0)
1984-91	-1.8 (1.4)	2.0 (0.3)	1.1 (0.9)

Beta=exponent of labor variable in Cobb-Douglas production function.
Wu and Wu used implicit deflator of industrial value added from the official GDP data to deflate output and capital stock.
In part B: I derived investment flow from net fixed assets date and used the perpetual depreciation inventory method to construct capital stock assuming a 5-percent depreciation rate. Factory-gate price index was used to deflate investment flow and output.

5. EXPLAINING THE GROWTH

The high rate of capital accumulation (the biggest contributor to Chinese growth) has its basis in the liberalization of a labor-surplus economy that has a high saving rate. Investment is highly profitable because the surplus labor prevented the real wage from rising significantly and the large pool of domestic saving prevented the interest rate from rising. The importance of the latter is seen in that household saving is about 23 percent of disposable income in China versus 21 percent in Japan, 18 percent for Taiwan, 16 percent for Belgium, 13 percent for West Germany and 8 percent for the United States (World Bank, 1990, Table 4.9).

Besides the existence of surplus agriculture labor, there were two other initial conditions that helped Chinese economic growth. The first supplementary initial condition was that the extent of China's central planning was much smaller than Russia's and Poland's. Qian and Xu (1993) noted that around 25 million commodities entered the Soviet economic plans, while in China, only around 1,200 commodities were included. The second supplementary condition was that China's reforms, unlike Polish and Russian reforms, did not start in a situation with large macroeconomic imbalances and a severe external debt crisis that required the implementation of an austerity program.

Another key factor behind China's impressive growth is its integration into the global economy. This factor operates through four channels. First, the access to international markets for labor-intensive manufactured goods accelerated the movement of labor out of low-productivity agriculture into high-productivity industry. Second, China could now buy modern technology (some of which were previously denied to China). Third, foreign direct investments increased the capital stock, transferred new technology, made available global distribution networks, and introduced domestic firms to more efficient management techniques. Fourth, the competition from international trade forced Chinese enterprises to be more efficient and innovative.

It should be noted that China's high household saving rate helped stabilize the economy beside enabling to a high rate of capital accummulation. It reduced inflation in the Chinese economy through two channels. First, the flow of savings through the banks reduced the need to print money to meet the excessive resource demand of the SOE sector. Second, as money was (until recently) the only form of financial saving in China, the high saving rate meant an increasing demand for money, hence dampening inflation pressure. This inflation-damping effect can be seen in the rise of the M2 to GNP ratio from 38 percent in 1979 to 106 percent in 1992.

6. CHALLENGES AND FUTURE GROWTH SCENARIO

Economic liberalization of China's surplus labor economy is the root cause of China's impressive growth. Economic efficiency improvements have been highest where economic liberalization has been bold (e.g. the decollectivisation of agriculture and the establishment of the COEs), and small when liberalization has been slow (e.g. the SOE sector). It therefore augurs well for China's economic future that the 15th Party Congress in September 1997 has decided to privatize 369,000 of China's 370,000 SOEs.

How compatible is the fixed investment rate of 32 percent of the Ninth Five-Year Plan with the 8 percent growth target?

Before answering this question, we note from the 1985-93 experience that an average investment-GDP ratio of 29 percent produced a capital stock growth rate of 11 percent.[25] Using the formula:

$$(dK/K) = (I/Y)(Y/K) - r$$

where:

K   = capital stock

I   = fixed investment

Y   = GDP

r   = depreciation rate

yields a capital-output ratio of 1.8 when a 5 percent depreciation rate is assumed.

I will assume that during the 9th 5-year plan:

(a) underdeflation of nominal output is corrected,

(b) labor reallocation effect = 1.2 percent

(c) net TFP growth   = 0.4 percent

(d) labor force growth   = 2.0 percent

(e) (K/Y)   = 2.0

(f) β = 0.5

(g) r   = 5.0 percent

The first result is that:

(I/Y) = 32 percent

will produce

(dK/K) = 11 percent

Then using:

(dY/Y) = capital contribution + labor contribution + TFP growth

---

25. Investment here refers only to fixed capital formation.

=   5.5   + 1.0   +   1.6

=   8.1 percent

>   8.0 percent target

On the basis of past growth, I would say that the Chinese government would almost surely achieve the 8 percent growth target. In fact, if the commitments of the Ninth Five-Year Plan to deepen reform in the enterprise sector and to increase China's opening to the world are fully implemented, I would venture the prediction that the 32 fixed investment rate would yield an average 9 percent growth rate because of TFP improvements of the magnitudes seen in the 1979-84 period.

In a way, the validity of this paper's analysis of China's growth record is supported by how close our estimated growth rate is to the target growth rate. The closeness suggests that the TFP growth rate assumed by the Chinese government is almost identical to the one I found. This may explain the radical enterprise reform program launched at the 15th Party Congress. The decision to privatise China's SOEs reflects, one, the official awareness that economic growth has been largely extensive in nature with little true technological progress, and, two, the official desire to switch the economy on to a more intensive growth path.

BIBLIOGRAPHY

Borensztein, Eduardo and Jonathan Ostry, 1996, "Accounting for China's Growth Performance," *American Economic Review*, May.

Chen Kuan, Wang Hongchang, Zheng Yuxin, Gary Jefferson and Thomas Rawski, 1988, "Productivity Change in Chinese Industry: 1953-1985," *Journal of Comparative Economics*, December, Vol. 12 No. 4, p.570-591.

Chow, Gregory, 1993, "Capital Formation and Economic Growth in China," *Quarterly Journal of Economics*, August.

Denison, Edward, 1974, *Accounting for United States Economic Growth 1929-1969*, Brookings Institution, Washington D.C.

Dollar, David, 1990, "Economic Reform and Allocative Efficiency in China's State-Owned Industry," *Economic Development and Cultural Change*, October, Vol. 39 No. 1, p.89-105.

Fan, Gang and Wing Thye Woo, 1996, "State Enterprise Reform as a Source of Macroeconomic Instability," *Asian Economic Journal*, November.

Granick, David, 1990, *Chinese State Enterprises: A Regional Property Rights Analysis*, University of Chicago Press.

Groves, Theodore, Yongmiao Hong, John McMillan, and Barry Naughton, 1994, "Autonomy and Incentives in Chinese State Enterprises," *Quarterly Journal of Economics*, Vol. 109 No. 1, February, pp. 185-209.

Groves, Theodore, Yongmiao Hong, John McMillan, and Barry Naughton, 1995, "Productivity Growth in Chinese State-Run Industry," in Fureng Dong, Cyril Lin and Barry Naughton, ed., *Reform of China's State-Owned Enterprises*, Macmillan, London.

Hu, Zuliu and Mohsin Khan, 1996, "Why is China Growing So Fast?" IMF Working Paper 96/75.

Huang Yiping and Xin Meng, 1995, "China's Industrial Growth and Efficiency: A Comparison between the State and the TVE Sectors," Research School of Pacific Studies, Australian National University, manuscript.

Jefferson, Gary, 1990, "China's Iron and Steel Industry Sources of Enterprise Efficiency and Impact of Reform," *Journal of Development Economics*, October, Vol. 33 No. 2, p.329-355.

Jefferson, Gary, Thomas Rawski and Yuxin Zheng, 1992, "Growth, Efficiency and Convergence in China's State and Collective Industry", *Economic Development and Cultural Change*, vol. 40, no.2, pp.239-266.

Jefferson, Gary, Thomas Rawski and Yuxin Zheng, 1994, "Comment on The Efficiency and Macroeconomic Consequences of Chinese Enterprise Reform by Woo, Fan, Hai and Jin," *China Economic Review*, Vol.5, No.2.

Jefferson, Gary, Thomas Rawski, and Yuxin Zheng, 1996, "Chinese Industrial Productivity: Trends, Measurement Issues, and Recent Developments," *Journal of Comparative Economics*, Vol. 23, pp. 146-180.

Li, Jingwen, 1992, "Productivity and China's Economic Growth," *The Economic Studies Quarterly*, Vol. 43 No. 4, December.

Naughton, Barry, 1994, "What is Distinctive about China's Economic Transition? State Enterprise Reform and Overall System Transformation," *Journal of Comparative Economics*, Vol. 18, No. 3, June.

Qian, Yingyi and Chenggang Xu, 1993, "Why China's Economic Reforms Differ: The M-form Hierarchy and Entry/Expansion of the Non-state Sector," *The Economics of Transition*, Vol. 1 No. 2, p.135-170, June.

Ren, Ruoen, forthcoming, *China's Economic Performance in International Perspective*, OECD, Paris.

Sachs, Jeffrey and Wing Thye Woo, 1994, "Structural Factors in the Economic Reforms of China, Eastern Europe and the Former Soviet Union," *Economic Policy*, April.

Sachs, Jeffrey and Wing Thye Woo, 1997, "Understanding China's Economic Growth," manuscript.

Woo, Wing Thye, Wen Hai, Yibiao Jin and Gang Fan, 1994, "How Successful Has Chinese Enterprise Reforms Been? Pitfalls in Opposite Biases and Focus," *Journal of Comparative Economics*, June.

World Bank, 1990, *China: Macroeconomic Stability and Industrial Growth under Decentralized Socialism.*

World Bank, 1992, *China: Statistical System in Transition.*

World Bank, 1994, *China: GNP per Capita.*

World Bank, 1996, *The Chinese Economy: Fighting Inflation, Deepening Reforms.* Wu, Harry Xiaoying and Yanrui Wu, 1994, "Rural Enterprise Growth and Efficiency," in Christopher Findlay, Andrew Watson and Harry Wu (eds.), *Rural Enterprises in China*, St. Martin's Press, New York, New York.

CHAPTER 3
CHINESE MANUFACTURING IN COMPARATIVE PERSPECTIVE

Adam SZIRMAI* AND Ruoen REN**

1. INTRODUCTION

In the 1980s and 1990s there was rapid growth in Chinese manufacturing. The increasing openness of the Chinese statistical system and the transition to the system of national accounts increased our knowledge and understanding of Chinese manufacturing performance. However, analyses based on official statistics tend to overestimate growth of output and productivity, while levels of output tend to be underestimated.

The present article is based on recent research on levels and trends of real output and labour productivity in Chinese manufacturing compared to those of the world productivity leader the USA.[1] It has three aims: 1. to make a benchmark comparison of real output and labour productivity in fifteen branches of manufacturing between China and the USA, and via the USA with other countries. 2. to present and to discuss estimates of growth rates of real output and labour productivity in these fifteen branches of manufacturing 3. to combine the benchmark comparisons and the time series in an analysis of relative labour productivity performance in Chinese manufacturing from 1980 to 1992. This allows us to say something about the dynamism of Chinese manufacturing.

* Professor of Development, Eindhoven university of Technology.

** Scholl of Business Management, Beijing University of Aeronautics and Astronautics.

1. See A. Szirmai and R. Ren , Rapid Growth without Catch Up. Comparative Performance in Chinese Manufacturing, 1980-1992, Eindhoven/Beijing April 1997. This paper presents a revision of estimates published in A. Szirmai and R. Ren, "China's Manufacturing Performance in Comparative Perspective", Groningen Growth and Development Centre, Research Memorandum 518 (GD 20), Groningen, 1995 and R. Ren, China's Economic Performance in an International Perspective, OECD Development Centre, Paris, 1997.

2. LEVELS OF OUTPUT

Levels of Chinese manufacturing output are underestimated for two kinds of resons: a. shortcomings of national statistics, b. the inadequacy of exchange rate conversions in international comparisons.

Shortcomings of national statistics include: a. Inadequate coverage of service output in health care, education, passenger transport, government administration and residential housing. This is a legacy of the material product system; b. Incomplete coverage of the booming private and semi-private sector of township and village enterprises. The data collection system is still based in part on administrative procedures characteristic of a centrally planned economy; c. Low valuation of output in Chinese currency due to pricing and subsidy conventions; d. Free or low cost provision of services to employees, leading to underestimation of value added in services; e. Understatement of agricultural value added.

It is well known that comparisons based on exchange rates substantially underestimate levels of national income in developing countries (see Kravis, Heston and Summers, 1982). Exchange rates do not adequately reflect differences of purchasing power of currencies between countries. Expenditure purchasing power parities (PPP) put total Chinese national income as much as 3.2 times as high as exchange rate comparisons (see Ren, 1997). The industry of origin PPPs for the manufacturing sector GDP, discussed in the following section, put China twice as high as exchange rate comparisons.

Methods

Using the *Chinese Industrial Census 1985* (Vol. I-X, 1987-1988) and the US *1987 Census of Manufactures,* we have made in total 67 matches of similar products or product categories for the benchmark year 1985.[2] For each product category, we can calculate unit values by dividing the value of output by output quantities. For each match one can calculate a unit value ratio. These unit value ratios are aggregated into purchasing power parities at higher levels, using quantity weights of either country. Thus we can derive purchasing power parities for specific industries, for 15 branches of manufacturing and for manufacturing as a whole. At each level of aggregation, one gets two PPPs, one at quantity weights of China, the other at quantity weights of the USA. We use the Fisher geometric average of the two PPPs as a summary measure. The Fisher purchasing power parities are calculated for the benchmark year 1985. These are used to convert

---

2. For more methodological detail the reader is referred to Szirmai and Ren (1995, 1997). These two papers also discuss the conceptual problems involved in a comparison between China and the USA. The methodology is the standard methodology of the International Comparisons of Output and Productivity Project ICOP (see Maddison and van Ark, 1994).

value added. The Purchasing Power Parities are reproduced in Annex Table A.1. The PPP for total manufacturing in 1985 is 1.45 yuan to the dollar against an exchange rate of 2.9 yuan to the dollar.

Estimates of Real Chinese GDP in Manufacturing

In 1985 gross domestic product in Chinese manufacturing was 231.6 billion Yuan.[3] Converting this figure to US dollars with our PPP gives a dollar value of 159.7 billion dollar. This represents 15.9 per cent of GDP at factor cost from the US Census. However, a substantial portion of manufacturing output is not covered by the Chinese census (see Table 1 for estimates of undercoverage). Using proportions of undercoverage in terms of gross output, we estimate that Chinese manufacturing GDP in 1985 was 18.4 per cent of GDP in US manufacturing.

Application of our own estimates of growth of manufacturing GDP in constant prices 1980-1992[4] to make a rough extrapolation to 1992, puts Chinese manufacturing GDP in 1992 at 24 per cent of US GDP. This, of course, has more to do with the sheer size of the Chinese economy, than with its productivity. UNIDO (1996, Table 1.1) estimates US manufacturing output in 1992 at 20.7 per cent of world manufacturing output. This suggests that China produced roughly four to five per cent of world output in 1992. Given the fact that the rate of growth of Chinese manufacturing has been substantially higher than that of OECD countries, China's share in world manufacturing GDP has gone up since 1992. In terms of contribution to world manufacturing output China has become one of the major world economies.

3. GROWTH RATES

Chinese growth rates tend to be overstated due to inadequate deflators. We have made estimates of growth from 1980 to 1992, using sectoral data on output from the 1993 *China Industrial Economic Statistics Yearbook* and producer price indices published for the first time in 1993 in the *1993 China Statistical Yearbook*. Use of these deflator's results in lower estimates of growth than the official ones (see Annex Table A.2). The compound growth rate of gross value of output in total manufacturing from 1980 to 1992 was 9.6 per cent per annum. The growth rate of net industrial output was 7.6 per cent per annum.[5]

---

3. Chinese net material product from the Census, Vol. 3, p. 90 ff, adjusted to the US census concept of value added, see Szirmai and Ren, 1997, Table 1.

4 . See Annex Table A2 for China and Szirmai and Ren, 1995, Table A.3 for the USA.

5. Net industrial output is a term deriving from the material product system. It roughly corresponds to net value added. For a discussion of conceptual differences between China and the US, see Szirmai and Ren, 1997.

Table 1: Coverage of Chinese Industry in the 1985 Census

	Number of Enterprises	Gross Output (mill. yuan)	Net Industrial Output (NIO) (mill. yuan)	Persons Engaged (Year-end)	GVO per person engaged (yuan)	GVO per person (as % of Row A)	NIO per person engaged (yuan)	NIO per person (as % of Row A)
A	Census: independent accounting enterprises, at township level and above,	358 701	843 472	273 366	66 045 000 e	12 771	100	4 144	100
	manufacturing	325 063	7 50 372	227 096	55 642 400 f	13 486	105.6	4 081	98.5
	mining, logging, utilities	33 638	93 100	46 567	10 402 600	8 950	70.1	4 476	108.0
B	Independent accounting enterprises below township level	4 722 069	99 422		27 910 400	3 562	27.9		
B1	Village collective (CSY, 1993; Census 85)	632 601	66 272		14 400 900 g	4 602	36.0		
B2	Rural cooperative (CSY 1993; Census 85)	741 664	15 175		5 191 200	2 923	22.9		
B3	Individual owned enterprises	3 347 804	17 975		8 318 300	2 161	16.9		
C	Total excluding non-independent accounting enterprises	5 080 770	9 42 894 b	na	93 955 400 g	10 036	78.6		
D	Non independent accounting enterprises	104 530	28 753		2 865 147 h	10 036	78.6		
E	Total including non-independent accounting enterprises	5 185 300 a	971 647 c	316 300 d	96 820 547	10 036	78.6	3 267	78.8

Source: unless indicated otherwise from Census, vol.3, p.367. (English version). All non-independent accounting enterprises are at township level and above, b gross output in all independant accounting systems, Census vol.3, p.9, c Census, vol.3, p.6 and CSY 1993, p. 367, d CSY 1993 p.30 and CIESY 1993 p.64, e Census, vol.8, p.2 ff. The census year-end employment figure is higher than the census year average figure (63,920,300), f Census, vol.8, p.2. The census year-end figure is higher than the census year average figure (53,849,200), g CSY 1993, p.76 and CIESY 1993, p.8 provides a figure of 83,490,000, h estimate of employment ssuming the same gross output per person as in total industry excluding the non-independent accounting sector.

It is interesting to note that the growth of net value added is 2 per cent lower than that of gross output and that the share of net value added in the gross value of output declined sharply over these twelve years from 34 to 27 per cent in industry and 31 to 25 per cent in manufacturing. Possible explanations for this trend include: 1. increasing specialisation and division of labour, including contracting out various activities to the service sector; 2. increasing inefficiency in the use of intermediate inputs; 3. changes in pricing conventions and statistical concepts.

If we compare these growth rates with growth rates for industry and manufacturing calculated directly from official constant price statistics (e.g SSB, 1988), or using official statistics (Wu, 1993), we find that our growth rates for domestic product are some 2.5 per cent lower (see Szirmai and Ren, 1995, tables 8-11).[6]

We have used these lower estimates in our extrapolation from our 1985 benchmark in the previous section. If we are too modest in our estimates, the share of China in world manufacturing in 1997 would be even greater than calculated above. Even the most modest growth rates point to great dynamism and rapid growth of output.

4. PRODUCTIVITY LEVELS

Using our purchasing power parities to make comparisons of real value added per person employed, results in an estimate of labour productivity in Chinese manufacturing of 6.2 per cent of the US level, for enterprises covered by the census of production. These results are reproduced in Table 2. The branch level productivity performance varies from a low of 3.6% in machinery and transport equipment to a high of 14.5 per cent in electrical machinery and equipment.

The causes of low productivity include low levels of capital intensity, which are to be expected in a labour surplus economy. They also include extensive labour hoarding and a very wasteful use of labour in enterprises. Casual observation suggests a considerable potential for productivity improvement through shake out. But the employment consequences of such policies would create political problems.

---

6. Another recent estimate of Chinese industrial GDP by Wu (1997) also results in slower growth than the official estimates, though his estimates are higher than ours.

Table 2: Gross Value Added (census concept) Per Personn Employed in China and the USA, 1985, in US$

	at Chinese Prices			at US Prices			Geom. Av.
	China	USA	China/USA (%)	China	USA	China/USA (%)	China/USA (%)
1+2 Food and beverages	5 530	109 634	5.0	4 095	68 121	6.0	5.5
1 Food Manufacturing	5 734	112 714	5.1	3 757	63 717	5.9	5.5
2 Beverages	4 806	88 825	5.4	5 295	97 878	5.4	5.4
3 Tobacco Products	7 967	65 939	12.1	21 612	170 171	12.7	12.4
4 Textile Mill Products	4 356	45 056	9.7	3 026	30 220	10.0	9.8
5 Wearing Apparel	2 957	34 798	8.5	2 134	25 398	8.4	8.4
6 Leather Products and Footwear	3 444	22 446	15,3	4 084	26 617	15.3	15.3
7 Wood Products, Furniture & Fixtures	2 716	58 670	4.6	1 569	33 871	4.6	4.6
8 Paper Products, Printing & Publishing	3 963	107 251	3.7	2 506	54 485	4.6	4.1
9 Chemical Products	7 897	150 673	5.2	6 834	92 694	7.4	6.2
10 Rubber & Plastic Products	4 756	169 277	2.8	5 851	46 315	12.6	6.0
11 Non-metallic Mineral Products	2 798	59 994	4.7	5 390	52 468	10.3	6.9
12 Basic & Fabricated Metal Products	5 820	30 943	18.8	3 906	46 870	8.3	12.5
13 Machinery & Transport Equipment	4 757	162 470	2.9	2 481	57 003	4.4	3.6
14 Electrical Machinery & Equipment	6 192	47 762	13.0	8 040	49 588	16.2	14.5
15 Other Manufacturing Industries	3 672	97 877	3.8	3 147	54 070	5.8	4.7
Total Manufacturing	4 768	97 639	4.9	4 133	53 209	7.8	6.2

Source: Gross value added from Szirmai and Ren, 1997, table 1 and 2; PPPs from annex table A1.

Low productivity would also seem to be related to the inflexibility of the labour market. Especially the state sector, which still accounts for a very substantial proportion of manufacturing employment and output, finds it very difficult to shed labour. Presently, the state sector of manufacturing is in serious trouble, with a high percentage of enterprises making a net loss.   Nevertheless, in 1985, labour productivity in the state sector was higher than in other sectors, probably due to economies of scale and higher capital intensity. Output per worker in the state sector was 25 per cent higher than that of workers in other enterprises covered by the industrial census of 1985.

Of the 5.2 million enterprises in industry (including mining, logging and manufacturing), only 358,701 enterprises with independent accounting systems at township level and above are covered adequately by the 1985 census. Table 1 illustrates the coverage of industrial activities. One of the interesting features of the Chinese industrial sector is the existence of great numbers of small enterprises with very few persons employed. In 1985 there were 3.3 million individual enterprises, with some 2.5 persons employed per enterprise. But the contribution of these enterprises to employment was very limited (8.3 million persons or 9 per cent of total employment in the sector). Most of employment and output was accounted for by the 358,701 larger enterprises, representing 68 per cent of all employment and 86.4 per cent of total output.

In terms of net output per person, labour productivity in the whole of industry was 79 per cent of that in the portion of industry covered by the census. Applying this ratio, to the manufacturing sector results in an even lower figure for comparative labour productivity, namely 4.9 per cent of the US level.

But it is also clear that low productivity cannot be explained by the existence of an enormous 'informal sector' in China, as in some other low-income economies. The main problem lies in the low levels of productivity in the most productive sector of larger enterprises.

5. EXPORT POTENTIAL INDICATED BY COMPARATIVE PRICE LEVELS (CPLS)

Underestimation of the relative size of Chinese national income due to the use of exchange rates leads to substantial overestimation of the share of exports in GDP. Sachs and Woo (1997) estimate Chinese exports at 24 percent of GDP in 1994, suggesting a very high degree of openness of the Chinese economy. However, if expenditure purchasing power parities were used to convert Chinese GDP into dollars, the share of foreign trade in national income would go down by a factor three.

Nevertheless, there has been very rapid export growth. Table 3 shows comparative price levels (CPLs, defined as PPPs divided by exchange rates) from 1985 to 1994. The fact that comparative price levels are so low is an indication of the price competitiveness of Chinese manufacturing and indicates a great potential for exports. This competitiveness is realised in spite of very low labour productivity level.

However, if the definition of competitiveness includes price competitiveness at degrees of productivity which will allow for decent remuneration of employees, than the Chinese economy cannot yet be seen as very compensating for low productivity with even lower wage levels.

6. DYNAMISM

The Chinese manufacturing sector manifests considerable dynamism. According to our estimates, which are lower than the official ones, value added is growing rapidly at 7.6 per year (see Annex table A2). Labour productivity is growing at 3.4 per cent per year (see Annex table A3).

In comparative terms, however, the gap *vis-à-vis* the USA stayed approximately the same between 1980 and 1992. Labour productivity was growing at about the same rate as that of the productivity leader, the USA. This means that in spite of its dynamism, Chinese manufacturing in the eighties was not yet catching up with the leading economies[7] (see Table 4).

7. COMPARATIVE PERFORMANCE IN THE ASIAN CONTEXT

In the Asian context China is doing worse than other Asian economies, such as South Korea and Taiwan which have been experiencing rapid productivity catch up since the middle eighties or Indonesia and India which are showing the first indications of catch up in the first half of the nineties (see Timmer and Szirmai, 1997).

In spite of its enormous size, the Chinese economy is presently still operating at very low productivity levels. It is big and at the same time stills 'less

---

7. The recent estimates of Chinese industrial growth from 1949-1994 by Harry Wu (1997) show more rapid growth of manufacturing between 1980-1992, than our estimates (9 per cent per year against 7.6 per cent). If we have underestimated growth, we may also have underestimated productivity growth and we would have to qualify our conclusion that there was no catch up in the eighties. However, there are no labour input series, corresponding to Wu's output series, so we cannot compare labour productivity estimates.

developed'. One could interpret the present phase of Chinese economic development as the laying of the foundations for future catch up. These foundations are not only indicated by sustained growth of output and employment, but also by substantial improvements in levels of human capital and improvements in life expectation and health indicators (see Szirmai, 1997, Chapter 5 and 6). When in due term declines in birth rates are transformed into slower growth of the labour force, the stage will be set for technological upgrading and productivity catch up in the course of the first half of the twenty first century.

Table 3: Comparative Price Levels, China/USA, 1980-1993 by Major Manufacturing Branch

	Food, Beverages Tobacco		Textiles Apparel Leather		Chemicals & Allied Products		Basic & Fabr. Metal Products		Machinery Equipment		Other Manufacturing		Total Manufacturing		Exchange Rate
	PPP	Price Level	PPP	Price Level	PPP	Price Level	PPP	Price Level	PPP	Price Level	PPP	Price Level	PPP	Price Level	
1985	1.32	4.0	1.37	46.5	1.50	51.2	0.99	33.8	1.78	60.5	1.17	39.9	1.45	49.4	2.94
1986	1.33	38.5	1.39	40.3	1.56	45.2	1.09	31.4	1.81	52.3	1.14	33.1	1.56	45.2	3.45
1987	1.44	38.7	1.49	40.1	1.77	47.5	1.15	30.0	1.87	50.2	1.35	36.2	1.64	44.1	3.72
1988	1.58	42.4	1.77	47.6	1.93	51.8	1.21	32.5	2.01	54.1	1.46	39.3	1.82	48.0	3.72
1989	1.74	46.3	2.12	56.2	2.27	60.3	1.46	38.7	2.35	624	1.56	41.5	2.06	54.7	4.77
1990	1.71	35.8	2.20	46.1	2.32	48.6	1.66	34.8	2.34	48.9	1.62	33.0	2.07	43.2	5.78
1991	1.77	33.3	2.27	42.6	2.39	44.0	1.97	36.0	2.37	44.4	1.68	31.6	2.18	40.0	5.32
1992	1.86	33.7	2.24	40.7	2.41	43.8	2.27	41.2	2.53	45.8	1.70	30.7	2.31	41.9	5.51
1993	2.06	35.8	2.33	40.4	2.61	45.2	3.54	61.5	3.02	52.5	1.84	31.0	2.82	49.0	5.76
1994	2.55	29.6	3.20	37.2	2.80	32.5	3.46	40.1	3.28	38.1	1.98	22.0	3.21	37.2	8.62

Note: Benchmark PPPs from annex table A1, extrapolated with price indices from Szirmai and Ren (1995). Exchange rates from IMF, *International Financial Statistics*, Washington, D.C., various issues.

Table 4: Comparative Productivity by Manufacturing Branch—China/USA, 1980-1992, USA=100

	Food & Beverages	Tobacco Products	Textile Mill Products	Wearing Apparel	Leather Products & Footwear	Wood Products Furniture, Fixtures	Paper Products Printing & Publishing	Chemicals, Petroleum & Coal Products	Rubber and Plastic Products	Non-Metallic Mineral Products	Basic & Fabricated Metal Products	Machinery and Transport Equipment	Electrical Machinery and Equipment	Other Manufacturing	Total Manufacturing
1980	6.2	8.2	12.4	7.1	15.9	4.9	3.9	7.9	7.6	7.4	11.7	3.3	9.6	4.8	6.3
1981	6.2	8.3	12.0	7.5	15.6	5.6	3.9	7.9	7.0	7.6	11.6	3.6	1.3	4.3	6.4
1982	5.8	9.3	11.1	7.8	15.1	5.3	3.9	7.5	7.1	7.7	13.2	3.9	1.4	4.5	6.6
1983	5.6	10.1	9.7	7.6	14.8	4.9	3.9	6.7	6.5	7.3	13.3	3.5	1.0	4.6	6.2
1984	5.6	10.3	9.5	8.0	14.0	4.6	4.0	6.3	6.4	7.3	12.7	3.4	12.7	4.0	6.0
1985	5.5	12.4	9.8	8.4	15.3	4.6	4.1	6.2	6.0	6.9	12.5	3.6	14.5	4.7	6.2
1986	5.8	11.2	9.0	8.3	17.5	4.1	4.1	5.8	5.9	6.6	12.8	3.4	13.7	4.2	6.0
1987	6.0	15.5	8.9	8.3	16.4	3.3	3.9	5.5	5.4	6.8	12.1	3.2	11.7	3.9	5.7
1988	6.4	17.3	8.9	8.2	15.2	3.5	4.1	5.5	5.8	7.1	12.5	3.3	12.9	3.5	5.8
1989	6.5	19.1	7.9	8.0	14.2	3.2	3.7	5.0	5.4	6.2	12.6	3.0	12.0	3.6	5.5
1990	6.5	22.3	7.2	7.7	14.7	3.2	3.6	5.2	5.3	6.2	10.7	2.7	10.4	3.3	5.3
1991	7.9	24.2	6.6	7.8	14.2	3.6	3.7	5.6	5.3	7.2	10.3	3.1	10.1	3.4	5.5
1992	8.2	26.3	7.0	8.9	12.2	4.3	4.1	6.3	5.7	8.7	11.9	3.7	10.4	3.7	6.2

Source : United States GDP from: US Dept. Of Commerce, *National Income and Product Accounts of the United States, 1929-1982*, Washington, DC, 1986; and US Dept. Of Commerce *Survey of Current Business*, January 1991, April 1991 and November 1992 issues ; Employment from NIPA, 1929-1982, Washington DC, 1986; NIPA, vol.2, 1959-1988, Washington DC, 1992 and US Dept. Of Commerce *Survey of Current Business*, Washington DC, Various issues. GDP and employment 1991 and 1992 from Survey of Current Business, July 1994. China: Net value added *from China Industrial Economic Statistics Yearbook, 1993*, pp. 142-154; deflators from SSB, *China Statistical Yearbook, 1993*, Beijing, 1993, table T7.24, pp. 238; employment from *SSB Industrial Economic Statistics Yearbook* of China, 1993. Benchmark productivity comparison from table 2.

BIBLIOGRAPHY

Kravis, I.B., A. Heston and R. Summers (1982), *World Product and Income*, Baltimore, Johns Hopkins University Press.

Maddison, A. and B. van Ark (1994), "The International Comparison of Real Product and Productivity", Groningen Growth and Development Centre, *Research Memorandum* 567 (GD-6), Groningen, April.

Ren, R. (1997), *China's Economic Performance in an International Perspective*, OECD, Paris (forthcoming).

State Statistical Bureau, (1987-88), Office of Leading Group of the National Industrial Census under the State Council, Peoples Republic of China, *Industrial Census 1985*, Vol. I-X, Statistics Printing House of China (in Chinese).

State Statistical Bureau (1988), *1988 Zhongguo Gongye Jingji Tongji Nianjian*, (1988 Industrial Economy Statistics Yearbook), Beijing.

State Statistical Bureau, (1993b). *1993 China Statistical Yearbook*, People's Republic of China, Beijing: Statistical Publishing House (in English).

State Statistical Bureau (1993c), *1993 Zhongguo Gongye Jingji Tongji Nianjian*, (1993 Industrial Economy Statistics Yearbook), Beijing.

Szirmai, A. and Ren, R. (1995), 'China's Manufacturing Performance in Comparative Perspective', Groningen Growth and Development Centre, *Research Memorandum* 518 (GD 20), Groningen.

Szirmai, A. and Ren, R. (1997), *Rapid Growth without Catch Up. Comparative Performance in Chinese Manufacturing, 1980-1992*, Eindhoven/Beijing April.

Szirmai, A. (1997), *Economic and Social Development. Trends, Problems, Policies*, Prentice   Hall, London/New York.

Timmer, M. and A. Szirmai (1997), *Growth and Divergence in Manufacturing Performance in South and East Asia*, Groningen Growth and Development Centre, Research Memorandum GD-37, Groningen, June 1997 (49. pp.).

UNIDO (1996), *International Yearbook of Industrial Statistics*, Vienna.

US Dept. of Commerce, (1990), Bureau of the Census, *US 1987 Census of Manufactures*, General Summary and Industry Series, Washington D.C.

Wu, H.X., (1993) "The `Real' Chinese Gross Domestic Product (GDP) for the Pre-Reform   Period, 1955-1977", in: *Review of Income and Wealth*, Series 39, No. 1, March, pp. 63-87.

Wu, H.X, (1997), *Reconstructing Chinese GDP According to the National Accounts Concept of Value Added: The Industrial Sector, 1949-1994*, Research Institute Systems Organisation Management, Research Report 97C24, Groningen.

APPENDIX

Table A1: Purchasing Power Parities and Price Levels by major Manufacturing Branch China/USA (PPP Yuan to the US$), 1985

	At US Quantity Weights	At Chinese Quantity Weights	Geometric Average	Relative Price level China (USA=100)
1+2 Food and Beverages	1.62	1.43	1.52	52.5
1 Food Manufacturing	1.77	1.53	1.64	56.7
2 Beverages	0.91	0.91	0.91	31.3
3 Tobacco Products	0.39	0.37	0.38	13.0
4 Textile Mill Products	1.49	1.44	1.47	50.5
5 Wearing Apparel (b)	1.37	1.39	1.38	47.5
6 Leather Products & Footwear	0.84	0.84	0.84	29.1
7 Wood Products, Furniture & Fixtures	1.73	1.73	1.73	59.7
8 Paper Products, Printing & Publishing	1.97	1.58	1.76	60.8
9 Chemical Products (incl.oil)	1.63	1.16	1.37	47.3
10 Rubber & Plastic Products	3.65	0.81	1.72	59.4
11 Non-metallic Mineral Products	1.14	0.52	0.77	26.6
12 Basic & Fabricated Metal Products	0.66	1.49	0.99	34.2
13 Machinery & Transport Equipment	2.85	1.92	2.34	80.6
14 Electrical Machinery & Equipment	0.96	0.77	0.86	29.7
15 Other Manufacturing Industries	1.81	1.17	1.45	50.1
Total Manufacturing, Census Weights (a)	1.84	1.15	1.45	50.2
Exchange Rate	2.9	2.9		

Note: (a) The PPP for total manufacturing is the weighted average of the PPPS of all manufacturing branches, weighted with value added weights. It can be based on census or national accounts weights, which give slightly different results.
(b) No sample industries in this branch. The PPP for wearing apparel is the weighted average of the PPPs for textiles and leather products and footwear.
Source: Sample industry PPPs from Szirmai and Ren, 1985.

Table A2: Chinese Gross Output and Net Industrial Output at Constant 1980 Prices, by Branch of Manufacturing 1980-1992 (million yuan)

Category of industry		1980	1984	1985	1986	1987	1988	1989	1990	1991	1992	Growth rate 1982-92
Food manufacturing	NIO	56.2	76.0	86.5	100.2	107.8	119.6	120.0	125.0	151.1	150.0	8.5
Beverages (a)	NIO	24.2	37.9	43.7	45.3	53.8	66.5	61.2	67.2	85.9	98.0	12.4
Tobacco (a)	NIO	53.3	95.3	102.4	119.9	133.5	149.4	153.4	173.2	178.3	186.8	11.0
Textile industry	NIO	199.8	231.1	274.2	303.1	317.1	328.2	314.3	302.5	296.5	325.5	4.2
Clothing industry	NIO	25.8	41.0	50.5	54.4	57.7	59.6	61.8	63.0	70.1	83.6	10.3
Leather, fur	NIO	13.4	15.5	19.2	22.2	25.1	24.7	23.7	26.1	29.4	29.4	6.8
Wood prod. and furniture (b)	NIO	17.3	21.7	22.4	22.7	18.6	18.4	16.7	16.1	18.3	21.1	1.6
Paper prod. and printing (c)	NIO	42.2	55.9	62.8	66.3	71.1	75.3	68.2	68.6	73.8	85.0	6.0
Oil refining, coal prod., coking (d)	NIO	71.0	83.1	86.7	95.2	98.2	99.4	87.9	81.4	88.7	101.6	3.0
Chemical industry, excl. Oil (e)	NIO	142.9	212.1	222.1	249.9	277.1	309.6	300.4	325.7	362.1	433.4	9.7
Rubber and plastic products (f)	NIO	51.5	69.9	76.9	77.9	81.8	91.3	89.5	91.2	100.1	115.9	7.0
Building mat./non metallic min.	NIO	80.5	114.8	129.4	138.2	141.3	152.2	134.5	130.4	151.8	198.2	7.8
Basic and fabricated metals (g/h)	NIO	168.9	213.6	233.2	249.6	273.6	287.9	285.1	253.0	256.7	320.4	5.5
Machinery & transp.equipment (i)	NIO	222.3	331.1	401.9	389.4	428.5	475.2	432.2	406.6	477.3	620.9	8.9
Electrical mach. & equipment (j)	NIO	77.6	134.8	171.2	164.7	181.0	213.6	217.3	203.4	227.2	248.5	10.2
Other industry (k) (l)	NIO	44.4	58.3	71.0	81.8	80.9	85.3	87.0	84.4	95.2	106.1	7.5
Total manufacturing	GO	4,134.0	5,976.9	6,864.0	7,392.0	8,255.8	9,199.9	9,200.6	9,364.6	10,473.0	12,437.8	9.6
Total manufacturing	NIO	1,291.2	1,792.4	2,054.0	2,180.9	2,347.0	2,556.2	2,453.1	2,417.7	2,662.9	3,124.2	7.6
Total industry	GO	4,702.5	6,731.0	7,660.2	8,256.1	9,177.9	10,284.9	10,388.6	10,673.5	11,878.5	13,959.8	9.5
Total industry	NIO	1,598.3	2,485.3	2,485.3	2,606.1	2,828.1	3,032.9	2,915.2	2,908.8	3,180.9	3,794.7	7.4

Sources: NIO: Net Industrial Output, GO: Gross Industrial Output. *China Economic Statistics Yearbook*, 1993, pp.142-154; Deflators calculated from SSB, *China Statistical Yearbook* 1993, Beijing, table T7.24, pp.238.

Note: (a) We used the price deflator for food products; (b) We used the price deflator for wood products, which we assume includes both loggin and wood products proper, (c) We used the price deflator for paper products; (d) We used the deflator for the industry, which, we assume, includes both crude oil production and oil refining; (e) Including medical industry and chemical fibres industry; (f) No separate index for rubber and plastics. We used the overall price index for industry; (g) Combining ferrous and non ferrous metals and fabricated metal products; (h) We used the index for the metallurgical industry, which probably refer to metal mining. This index shows very rapid price increases. Thus the series may understate growth; (i) We used the price deflator for machinery; (j) Including electronic and communication equipment. There was no separate deflator for this branch. We used the overall price index as a deflator; (k) We combined cultural products, arts and crafts, measurement instruments and other the ICOP category other, (l) We used the price deflator for cultural products for cultural products and art and crafts and the overall price deflator for instruments and other.

Table A3: Chinese Net Value Added Per Personn Employed by Branch of Manufacturing 1980-1992 (in constant 1980 Yuan)

Category of Industry (ICOP BRANCH)	1980	1985	1986	1987	1988	1989	1990	1991	1992	Compound growth
Total industry	3179	3763	3819	3875	4034	3863	3796	3994	4682	3.3%
1+2 Food and Beverages	2976	3087	3222	3362	3761	3704	3878	4642	4822	4.1%
1 Food manufacturing	2587	2702	2855	3018	3281	3309	3397	4008	3971	3.6%
2 Beverage manufacturing (a)	4578	4302	4329	4357	5103	4836	5262	6430	7174	3.8%
3 Tobacco processing	39577	42332	45995	49975	52548	52186	58605	57435	58380	3.3%
4 Textile industry	4196	3802	3760	3718	3661	3441	3258	3094	3482	-1.5%
5 Clothing industry	1907	2438	2543	2652	2751	2847	2765	2887	3388	4.9%
6 Leather, fur and man. Products	2229	2224	2390	2569	2508	2431	2551	2666	2610	1.3%
7 Wood products and furniture	1551	1486	1338	1205	1207	1105	1052	1192	1409	-0.8%
8 Paper and printing	2526	2858	2852	2846	2910	2637	2596	2684	3029	1.5%
9a Oil refining and coal products	19860	18972	18072	17215	15961	13196	11742	11121	12107	-4.0%
9b Chemical industry, excl. Oil refin	4191	5186	5451	5730	5995	5655	5846	6171	7172	4.6%
9 Chemical industry, total	24051	24158	23523	22944	21956	18851	17587	17293	19279	-1.8%
10 Rubber and plastic products	3815	3965	3879	3795	4037	3959	3912	4060	4620	1.6%
11 Non-metallic minerals	1766	1948	1930	1912	2026	1861	1866	2114	2755	3.8%
12 Basic and fabricated metals	3392	3888	4009	4133	4204	4104	3599	3593	4367	2.1%
13 Machinery and transport equipment	2167	3394	3411	3427	3710	3417	3194	3636	4662	6.6%
14 Electric machinery and equipment	2767	4702	4597	4494	5157	5234	4742	4969	5343	5.6%
15 Other industry	2457	2910	2793	2680	2859	2918	2744	2964	3346	2.6%
Total manufacturing	3084	3697	3744	3790	4006	3847	3736	3963	4610	3.44%

Sources : Net Value added (net industrial output) from Table A2. Employment from *China Economic Statistics Yearbook*, 1993, pp. 90 ff.

CHAPTER 4
THE REALITY AND THE MYTHS OF CHINA'S OPENING

Françoise LEMOINE *

China's success in world markets is yet another "Asian miracle", which both frightens and fascinates Westerners. In the last 15 years, China has tripled its share of world trade, and leads the emerging countries in certain sectors such as toys and clothing. If statistics are to be believed, the country is now very open and largely geared to exports. But reality is quite different: the spectacular rise of China in world trade is essentially due to a huge relocation of Asian industrial production, while the domestic market remains relatively closed. European companies are very well placed within this latter market, leading their Asian counterparts by a long way and even the Americans. Presently, the real challenge is focused on China's membership negotiations with the World Trade Organisation.

1. FOREIGN TRADE AND THE DOMESTIC MARKET

The expansion of China's international trade since 1980 has, without doubt, been one of its greatest successes. International trade statistics credit China with an annual average of 15% growth in its foreign trade, between 1981 and 1995. Yet, these developments also solicit a certain degree of perplexity: at 40%, the degree of openness of the Chinese economy, measured as the sum total foreign trade (exports and imports) relative to GDP, is exceptionally high for a country of its size and level of development; this degree of openness being twice that of India, and three times that of Brazil. China also stands out because of the very high share of manufactured goods in its exports: more than 80%, as opposed to less than 60% in India and Brazil. How has this occurred?

The answer lies to a large extent in the relocation of Asian industries to China. About half of China's foreign trade in volume terms currently stems from international assembly and sub-contracting operations, and it is these operations that have been almost exclusively responsible for the spectacular expansion of Chinese exports since 1980 (see Graph 1). Such an analysis sheds new light on rise of Chinese exports, their product composition, as well as the strategies and positions of China's partners.

---

* Senior Economist at the CEPII.

Graph 1 - China in World Trade   in %

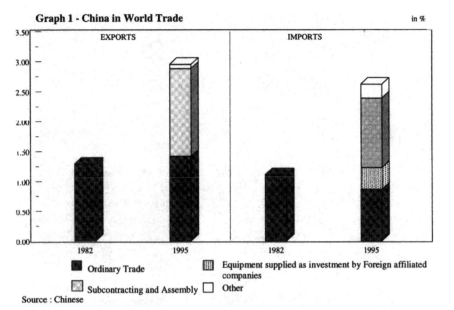

Source : Chinese

Within international assembly and sub-contracting operations exports and imports are linked: Chinese companies transform and assemble imported intermediate products and components for re-export. Such trade is marked by a number of characteristics which distinguish it from other trade. To begin with, it benefits from a specific customs regime, and hence figures in customs' statistics. However, neither the intermediate, imported products nor the finished goods normally enter the domestic market or are in competition with local products. Thus, such trade is completely isolated from the rest of the Chinese economy, yet it is highly integrated in the international production and trade networks of foreign firms.

Assembly and processing trade was non-existent prior to the reforms opening up China in 1979, but its real expansion did not begin until the second half of the 1980s, under the combined impact of Chinese measures and the evolution of the Asian economies. In 1987, the Chinese government announced a development strategy favouring export-oriented industries, and made the transformation and exportation of imported goods the key to industrialisation in its coastal regions. Within an overall customs' regime of high tariffs, the exemption of duties for goods to be re-exported turned out to be a powerful stimulant. At the same time, Asia's industrialised economies were experiencing higher wage costs, thus altering their traditional comparative advantages in labour-intensive industries; a phenomenon reinforced in Taiwan by the re-evaluation of its currency in 1987. The convergence of these trends sparked a vast relocation of industrial capacity from Hong Kong, and Taiwan, as well as from Japan to China, which has been responsible for the explosive growth of Chinese trade. Currently, 44% of Chinese imports and 49% of exports are linked to the transformation of imported goods.

The other area of Chinese foreign trade, which truly stems from domestic supply and demand, has hardly expanded more quickly than world trade as a whole. Subject to the usual customs' tariffs, such trade is classified as "ordinary" in official Chinese statistics, with exports growing moderately and imports weakly. Thus in 1995, these exports accounted for about 1.4% of world trade, as opposed to 1.3% in 1982, while the world share of imports fell from 1.1% to 0.9%. Thus only a small share of total imports (about one third) is destined for Chinese companies and consumers. To these imports should be added capital transfers in kind, in the form of capital equipment supplied by foreign companies setting up subsidiaries and joint-enterprises in China, be it to supply the domestic market or assembly for exports. Such imports were exempt from customs' duties up until November 1995. If assembly and sub-contracting operations are excluded from foreign trade, then the degree of openness of the Chinese economy is of more modest proportions, with foreign trade being equivalent to 20% of GDP.

Total Chinese foreign trade is thus made up of two, heterogeneous structures: the composition of the supply and demand for products in re-export industries is thus very different from that characterising ordinary industries (see Table 1).

By their nature, the imports geared to assembly and sub-contracting operations take up more raw materials and intermediate products than is the case for other imports. The exports arising from these operations also generate more finished products, though China does not master all the production processes of such goods. Re-export industries have been at the leading edge of the rapid growth in manufactured exports, especially in new industries like electrical goods. In this market segment, Chinese exports are characterised by the strong concentration on a small number of products, which in turn explains China's intense specialisation in world markets (ten product categories out of the 71 making up the CHELEM[1] classification account for 70% of sales). For the textile and electrical goods industries, intra-industry trade (i.e. simultaneous exports and imports) reflects the intensity of China's vertical division of labour and the international segmentation of the productive process.

---

[1] CHELEM: databank of international trade and the world economy maintains by the CEPII.

Table 1 : The Weight of Different Trade Segments in Total Exports and Imports in 1995

Total exports = 100   Total imports = 100   *in %*

| | Sub-contracting and assembly | | Ordinary trade | | Foreign affiliated companies |
	Exports	Imports	Exports	Imports	Imports
Total	49.5	44.2	48.0	32.8	19.6
Food, agriculture, raw materials	2.0	5.2	10.9	7.5	1.0
Chemicals, rubber	2.8	8.0	5.5	4.8	1.4
Wood, paper, furniture, toys	4.6	2.3	3.3	1.1	0.5
Textiles	16.5	10.9	16.1	1.0	0.2
Metals	3.5	4.3	3.0	2.6	1.3
Machinery	4.2	2.2	2.8	7.3	11.0
Electrical Machinery	12.7	9.7	3.0	5.8	2.7
Transport equipment	1.8	0.2	0.8	2.5	1.1
Construction materials, other	1.4	1.3	2.6	0.3	0.3

* Excluding assembly. 75% are capital investments.

Sources: Chinese Customs.

The structure of "domestic" exports has also evolved over the last 15 years, as manufactured goods are now predominant. But agricultural products, food and raw materials are still important to exports. Imports for the domestic market reflect the high demand for capital equipment (machines and transport equipment making up half of imports), on top of which should be added the contributions of foreign investors.

2. EUROPE LEADS IN THE DOMESTIC MARKET

The respective positions of China's main partners in these two areas of trade are very different. Essentially, exports from the Newly Industrialised Countries (NICs - Hong Kong, South Korea and Taiwan) are not destined for the domestic market, but follow instead from relocation strategies geared towards third markets or re-importation (to home markets). Japanese exports follow the same pattern, though with some nuance. In contrast, Europe and the United States are the top suppliers for the domestic market, and are little present in assembly and sub-contractor trade. This is due to geographic distance and/or sectoral specialisation which are less favourable to integrating China into a segmented production process

Graph 2: The Nature of Chinese imports by Trading Partners in 1995

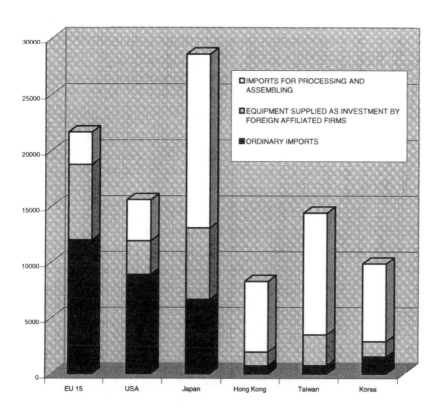

Thus, the countries of the European Union account for 28% of imports destined for China's domestic market (excluding capital brought in by foreign companies). They thus lead the United States (21%) and Japan (15%). The predominance of Europe stems in general from the manner in which its exports are well adapted to the needs of China's domestic modernisation. The European Union is particularly strong in mechanical engineering, where European companies supply about half of China's ordinary imports of machinery, electrical equipment and vehicles. US exporters are especially strong in raw materials (cereals: 42% and fertiliser: 43%), as well as in precision instruments (37%). Japan is the only Asian country present on the domestic market, though lagging behind Europe and the United States in all products. Other Asian companies have not yet entered the domestic market, which is protected by tariffs, and even more so by non-tariff barriers. Looking at total imports, excluding those for assembly and sub-contracting (i.e. drawing together ordinary imports and those linked to capital contributions by foreign companies), then Europe still comes out ahead (with 25% of imports), but Japan has a slightly larger share than the United States (respectively 18% and 17% of imports).

Asian companies have followed a strategy of extending their production and trade networks to China, aimed more at Chinese workers than at Chinese consumers. More than half of Japan's exports to China, and over 70% of exports from Hong Kong, South Korea and Taiwan are geared to being transformed and re-exported. Together, these four countries account for over 80% of China's assembly and sub-contracting imports. The sectoral and relocation strategies reflect their different levels of industrial maturity: Japanese companies relocate production mainly in mechanical and electrical engineering, whereas Taiwan and South Korea have above all transferred production capacities related to first-generation, labour-intensive industries (textiles-clothing, plastic goods and various manufactured items).

3. THE ESSENTIAL ROLE OF FOREIGN INVESTORS

Whatever the strategy pursued by China's partners (seeking out markets or looking for production cost advantages), foreign direct investment has played a decisive role in trade flows. Foreign companies investing in China generate about half of all Chinese imports (see Table 2). About 60% of Chinese imports in machinery and capital equipment are linked to foreign investment: it is easier to set up production capacity in China than to sell capital equipment to domestic producers. This strategy allows China to associate capital equipment imports with the transfer of know-how. For European companies, such investments are a way of getting a foothold in the Chinese market. In contrast, the role of foreign-owned companies is less important to American exports: US sales include a relatively important share of products which come under " arm's length " trade (cereals and fertilisers).

Table 2: The Role of Foreign-Owned Companies in Chinese Imports, in 1995

In % of total imports from each partner, in each product category

	UE 15	United States	Japan	Hong Kong	Taiwan	South Korea	World
All products	40.5	33.2	58.7	57.9	70.7	59.8	47.7
Machinery	47.5	47.1	64.3	64.9	85.2	81.7	59.2
Electrical equipment	30.0	39.1	62.3	62.1	66.0	77.7	53.6
Vehicles	58.2	53.5	27.6	54.1	65.4	42.5	49.5

Sources: Chinese Customs.

For Asian companies, foreign investments are the basis of production relocation, and intra-company trade dominates assembly and sub-contracting operations[1]. Foreign companies in China account for nearly 60% of exports, and about two-thirds of imports linked to assembly and sub-contracting. When these are managed by foreign-owned companies, such operations only provide China with a relatively limited trade surplus (the gap between imports and exports): 13% on average, as opposed to 25% for all assembly and sub-contracting operations taken together. This may be interpreted in various ways: either foreign companies are specialised in industries with low value-added; or they use biased transfer prices in intra-company trade; or they sell a share of products geared to being re-exported on the domestic market; or lastly they use less local inputs than do Chinese companies present in the same sector.

The rise of Chinese manufacturing exports in Western markets, at the expense of the Asian NICs, must be examined in the light of the role which companies from these countries are henceforth playing in China's overall exports. There is however limits to this strategy, stemming from the saturation of outlets for China's down-market goods, as well as from the rising competition by more recent emerging countries. Furthermore, industrialisation from re-export trade in China is deepening the gap between the coastal regions, which are developing rapidly, and inland China, which is still on the sidelines of internationalisation. These factors explain the recent adjustments in Chinese trade policy, which is becoming more selective with respect to foreign investment, seeking notably to slowdown the relocation of certain labour-intensive industries and to encourage foreign investment in sectors that meet China's domestic, modernisation needs.

The situation in China is thus paradoxical, as international trade (in exports and imports) is growing very quickly, while the domestic economy is only opening up slowly. Indeed, the concentration of trade has led to regions in the interior, and more generally whole areas of industry (dominated by state enterprises, of which half recorded losses in 1996) being protected from international trade. Thus the competitiveness of Chinese industries in world markets does not determine the capacity of local industries to stand up to international trade in domestic markets.

Along with its negotiations to enter the World Trade Organisation, China has started a progressive liberalisation of its domestic market. In April 1996, it reduced the average level of customs duties from 32% to 24%, and in October China announced that this level would fall to 15% by the year 2000. The question of isolated " tariff peaks " still remains open, as prohibitive rates remain on certain goods (notably cars), which are of particular interest to China's main trade partners. In addition, and despite the reduction in the number of

---

[1] It should be noted that the role of foreign direct investment from Hong Kong is over-estimated, as far as it includes " re-cycled " capital investments from mainland China, which benefit from the preferential conditions provided to foreign investors in China.

import licences in April 1996, non-tariff barriers remain a powerful instrument for controlling imports. The right of foreign companies to establish themselves in China to supply the domestic market with goods and services is also subject to official authorisation, and may only take place within a broad policy of import substitution pursued by the authorities.

Until now, negotiations with the WTO have not granted China the delays it has asked for conforming to the organisation's trade regime. With the new flexibility shown in both the American and Chinese positions at the end of 1996 a compromise is in the offing, which will provide China with a long period of transition, but only in sectors deemed as particularly " sensitive ". This selective approach appears to conform with the pragmatism of the Chinese authorities concerning reforms, and would allow them to retain certain priorities in their trade policy. Ultimately, however, the European countries, which presently benefit from the existing protection of the domestic market, will come under greater competitive pressure: the liberalisation of imports and foreign direct investment will lead the Asian countries to intensify their efforts to penetrate the domestic market. As for the uniformisation of customs conditions throughout China (which assumes the suppression of privileges accorded to the special economic zones), it runs up against the opposition of the coastal areas that have based their prosperity on such privileges, though it remains a long-term goal of the central authorities. The entry of China into the WTO thus raises not only questions about trade policy formulated in Beijing, but also touches on Beijing capacity to impose its disciplines over the diverging interests of the provinces.

CHAPTER 5
IS THE TRANSITION UNDER CONTROL? GRADUALISM AND MACROECONOMIC POLICY

FAN GANG [*]

Are Chinese economic reforms under control? Is any strategy being carried out? Three issues will be presented to answer these questions.

1. Is there a reform strategy in China and are the Chinese authorities using a model different from the one used by other developing countries?

2. Is the reform under control?

3. How has macroeconomic management been carried out in China? Is the cyclical movement going to be explosive?

1. MODELS AND STRATEGIES

When talking about models and strategies, we should distinguish two things:

- Is there a reform policy or a reform model that has been adopted officially?
- What is happening in the reality?

1) The Chinese government is obviously pursuing some objectives. Every major party congress or change in leadership leads to the announcement of a new policy model. But the most important is that the model and the strategies have been changing along with the changes of the reality in China.

The changes in objective models announced by government happened as follows.

At the beginning of the reforms in late 1970, the objective was to have a planned economy with some elements of "commodity regulation". A couple of years later it changed for the combination of planning and market, a planned

---

[*] Director of the National Institute of Economic Research, Beijing.

economy supplemented by market regulations. Then it changed again in 1993 for the formula of "socialist market economy".

Table 1: The Evolution of Reform Objective

Period	Desired Endpoint Upon Completion of Reform
Pre-1979	A planned economy under the law of exchange value
1979 to October 1984	A planned economy supplemented by market regulations
October 1984 to October 1987	A planned commodity economy
October 1987 to June 1989	An economy where the state regulates the market and the market regulates the enterprises
June 1989 to 1991	An economy with organic integration of planned economy and market regulations
1992 to present	A socialist market economy with Chinese characteristics

However, the definition of a "socialist market economy" has itself been changing. At the beginning it was defined as the "predomination by state-owned enterprises with some market forces". Then it changed to the "leading role" of state sector in the economy. Then it changed again to the current model which is a combination of the state sector and the private sector. It is probably going to change one more time this year, at the party congress, with a change in the definition of the way state assets are managed; namely, the share-holding companies can be used for any kind of enterprise. State assets can be sold and state enterprises can be converted into share-holding systems with capital from the private sector. The whole definition of the objective model has been evolving in the past 18 years, along with the progress of reforms and development.

2) The models followed by China in reality

In the long run the fundamentals of the market system will be developed in Chinese economy, though it will be with Chinese characteristics, depending on its history, its past system, its culture, its value system.

A lot of questions have been raised by the current situation of the Chinese economy. China is still in an early stage of development of a market. China has started its marketisation in another way compared to other developing countries, because it started from a planned economy. China is not only a developing country but also an economy in transition, which refers therefore to the process leading from a planned economy to a market economy. This is different from the situation in other Asian countries. Consequently the development model may not be different from the one used in other countries but China's past is different, and the pattern of the transition period may be different.

The economic transition in China is also different from that in East-European countries, which already had a highly industrialised centralised economy, before the reforms. Indeed, before the reform, China was a combination of a rural society and a planned economy. That sets different initial conditions.

Last but not least, in China, like in any other country, the "strategy" is the outcome of political and economic environment, which comes out of the conflicts of groups. Consequently, even if the government has objective models the results still depend on the real situation of the economy and on the influence of the different political groups and of their conflicts. The Chinese are pragmatic. There are a lot of ideological constraints, but the majority of government officials are looking for pragmatic and practical solutions to the problems.

2. IS CHINESE REFORM UNDER CONTROL?

Chinese reform has mainly been marked by the decentralisation and deregulation of the economic system. After 18 years, the Chinese economy and Chinese society are really decentralised in a way that government has decentralised the decision-making powers to individuals: to the private sector and to the regions, to the cities and to the local governments. It is no longer a centralised system and the reforms themselves are no longer to be a centralised process.

Since 1993, some local governments have initiated the reforms of small state enterprises. State assets have been sold or state enterprises, as a whole, have been sold or merged with other enterprises or sold to the workers and converted to employee shareholder corporations.

In the past 3-4 years this process actually has accelerated on a large scale in many local areas. In some provinces a large percentage of enterprises has been privatised. In Guandong province and in Shandong province, 70% or 80% of small state enterprises at the county level or at the city level have been reformed. This process has actually been a "bottom-up" process, initiated by local people and observed by the central government without central regulation, except for the regulation of the valuation of state assets. Central government has not stopped the process. It has only watched carefully what is going on.

Recently (only at the end of 1996), this process was officially complemented by the central government. In this sense, the process is not under the control of the central government; it is under the control of the local government.

It was initiated by the local government, and the central government let the experiment develop in many local areas. If something had gone wrong it would have been stopped. If something appears to be good it will be used as a model for other areas.

Such local experiments and the bottom-up process are features of the current stage of China's reform. In some sense it is out of the control of the central government, but in another sense it is a way to use the market to decentralise and to develop the country. If things were only going to take place after some central government regulation had been formulated, the ·process would be more complicated and take much longer, than is the case with local initiative.

China is so big. Its conditions are so different from one place to another! In some coastal regions the percentage of non-state enterprises is higher, making the reform easier, but in the Northeast and Northwest regions it is more complicated. In the central spheres, there are more political constraints and conflicts between the different groups to face. Consequently, it is more complicated for the central government to make any comprehensive reform package.

This kind of reform process can appear to be and actually is chaotic, but the central government still exercises some control over local practices. Central government now plays some role as a brake. Things are going forward but if something is going wrong, if a conflict becomes to extreme, the government will intervene. In this sense the central government acts to prevent the worst from happening and gives the decision-making power to local governments to initiate and experiment some reforms.

This process can be expected to continue for the next couple of years.

3. MACROECONOMIC MANAGEMENT

China just comes through a business cycle. In 1992-1993 the economy overheated. In 1994, inflation was at the highest level of the past 18 years of reform. In 1993, central government started to adopt some restrictive macroeconomics policy. And after 3 years, inflation came down to 6% 1996. At the moment there is zero inflation. For a developing country, inflation may be too low now and, with $120 billions, the foreign reserves may be too high.

Anyway with the inflation being so low, China is at the bottom of the cycle. The Chinese central government has been weak in implementing monetary and fiscal policy. The Chinese economy is still very vulnerable to overheating with a large state sector. But the Chinese central government still has shown that it has some control on the macroeconomics.

Today the Chinese government still has three macroeconomic tools to implement its economic policy, when most other countries have two instruments: monetary policy and fiscal policy

China has a third tool: its investment policy.

Over the past three years, the most effective policy has neither been fiscal policy nor monetary policy. Investment is controlled by the central government through the planning commission. That is why the major projects have to be approved by the planning commission. In this way, the government controls the total volume of investments which become a major policy instrument. It means that the Chinese government still uses an administrative tool for macroeconomic control policy.

Why are Chinese doing this?

The reason is that there is still a large state sector. For the state sector, interest rate controls and monetary policy do not work, so that only administrative regulation can control its behaviour, especially its investment behaviour. That is why when things go out of control, when inflation rises, the government falls back on administrative instruments which are effective.

Effectiveness of administrative policy is declining with the growth of the market in Chinese economy. It is diminishing, but it is still in use.

Compared to other economies in transition, it seems that the existence of a kind of political authority is helpful to prevent the economy from going exploding.

CHAPTER 6
DIVERGING VIEWS ABOUT ECONOMIC REFORM IN CHINA'S POLITICAL STRUCTURE

André CHIENG[*]

Without going into a detailed analysis of the policies of the Communist Party, a certain number of observations may be made based on the usual information available. The latter demonstrates that China has experienced extraordinary economic growth since 1978, following the well-known "open door" and liberalisation policy of Deng Xiaoping. The most impressive results have been obtained in recent years. This was especially so in 1996, when it seems (according to official statistics) that China achieved what my economics professors called the impossible triangle, namely that of the restraint of inflation combined with high growth and balanced trade. Indeed in 1996, inflation stood at 6%, growth reached 9.7% and foreign trade recorded a surplus of about $10 billion. All this shows that China's macroeconomic indicators are very impressive. What are the problems which may be encountered? It is clear that China's difficulties are also very important, and that they will lead to a number of divergences in economic policy, which China will have to adopt. This is entirely normal, as the reforms in China started in 1978, fully eighteen years ago. The first reforms were the easiest to implement and the least controversial. Problems generating greater debate have been met in the later stages of reform, given the increasing complexity of the Chinese economy. Four subjects for debate are raised in this paper.

The first debate and the first divergence are well known, centring on inflation and growth. This is a problem all economies face, including China. Deng Xiaoping's position on the matter was known, as he favoured growth before price stability. In his famous speech in 1992, and during his journey to Southern China, he wanted to re-launch the economic reforms, stating that they were not proceeding sufficiently quickly. In fact, he wanted to say that it was absolutely vital for growth to be re-launched. This is understandable, given that strong growth was the principal justification for his policy. Deng Xiaoping used to say that, according to Mao and customary Chinese wisdom, practice is fundamentally the only criteria of truth, while rapid growth in China bore out the correctness of his policy. To be sure, he also noted that inflation is a problem, and that measures should be taken accordingly. But for him growth was of

---

[*] Chairman, Asiatique Européenne de commerce.

primary importance. It appears that this policy was pursued for a certain time, but changed quite rapidly, especially in 1993. Overall, it is perhaps possible to say that China entered the market economy definitely on the 1 July 1993. Why the 1 July 1993? Because at this point Mr. Zhu Rong Ji took over as head of the People's Bank of China, and as you know, it was from here that he instituted a real policy of what is known throughout the world as macroeconomic control. The results are known to us, and constitute a remarkable success, all the more so, as growth does not seem to have suffered, even when the criticisms of the reliability of the statistics are taken into account. It must therefore be asked whether this success may be applied and achieved in other areas.

The second point concerns the other major debate: that of centralisation-decentralisation. One of the pillars of Deng's reform was decentralisation. To begin with, decentralisation was totally incontestable, as it implied "the necessity of giving initiative to the Provinces, the necessity of shortening the decision-making process, and the necessity of getting closer to reality on the ground". This has been demonstrated in the presentation by Mr. Fan Gang. We have seen the benefits of decentralisation. Now it is time to look at some of the disadvantages. Two stand out in particular. The first concerns the sharing out of resources between the Centre and the Provinces. From this point of view, we know that China is in an exceptional situation. Using the figures for 1995 (which are quite rough), it would seem that the split of tax resources between the Centre and the Provinces is 40% to 60% respectively. This is quite abnormal, as most large countries throughout the world are in the opposite situation. I am not even talking of France, where the situation is closer to 80-20%. Most other countries tend to have a 60-40% ratio. This is one of China's major problems. Another important problem, which can perhaps be linked to the dialectics of centralisation-decentralisation, is the irrational structure of the economy. The reforms have introduced this decentralisation, but they have not been followed through, in particular with respect to the separation of the State and enterprises, and in some cases the drawbacks of both are cumulated. This is the case in the provinces, and can be demonstrated by various examples. Thus, the car industry was adopted as a key industry in 1994. Yet, what is to be observed? Twenty-three provinces and cities entered the automobile industry, generating substantial, theoretical output capacity of 5,700,000 vehicles per year, by the year 2000, even though demand is only expected to run at 2,700,000. The result is that capacity is used extremely badly. For example, in the Chang Chun plant, which is the largest in China, the capacity utilisation rate for average vehicles is only 62%, for light vehicles 50%, and as little as 45% for particular vehicles like sedans. Other figures show, for example, that a little over 30 factories produce less than 100 vehicles per year. As for the large automobile factories (i.e. the Dong Feng and FAW groups), their production capacity is in the order of several hundred thousand (200,000 or 300,000 vehicles), which compares with a capacity of around 10 million for the world's major producers like Ford and General Motors. The gap between the two is thus very clear. Lastly, the cumulative capital and the cumulative turnover of the 500 largest

Chinese companies hardly surpasses that of the two or three largest American firms.

The third problem, which is often, put forward, concerns public enterprises. It has become particularly acute, as it is practically the primary difficulty facing the present government. Based on World Bank data, public enterprises in 1995 accounted for nearly 34% of industrial output, 73% of investment, and fully 70% of urban employment. These figures are absolutely typical of China's problems, and as a result public enterprises lose money. According to the World Bank, such losses represent between 2.4% and 5.3% of GDP, not including indirect aid through concessionary interest rates. When all these factors are drawn together, it would appear that the losses of public enterprises amount to 10% of GDP. How has this come about? This process is quite easy to understand. China presently has an extremely important non-state sector, accounting for the majority of output. But, what is amazing is that this sector has emerged without any real privatisation. There has been no great privatisation movement, as may be observed in the other transition economies. How has this private sector developed? On the one hand it has followed from the creation of companies based on small enterprises, and on the other hand it has followed the rampant privatisation of public SMEs. Jiang Zemin recently described this policy by stating that "for public enterprises, the [state] will control the large ones and let the smaller ones loose". In this case "letting the smaller ones loose" means "rampant privatisation", through a system of responsibility contracts. But, such contracts are only applied to enterprises capable of being reformed and which are well managed. "Loser" companies, or those which could not feasibly be privatised have remained in the public sector. Hence it is not surprising to find that the public sector is carrying much labour, and loosing money. The sector invests enormously, using substantial financial resources. Given that the policy of macroeconomic control reduces the financial resources available, this must surely lead to the crowding-out of private companies from available capital.

The fourth problems hinges on the openness of the market. This is one of the pillars of Deng's reforms, and has been pursued in various ways, the two most important being: first, the introduction of modern production and management methods; and second the stimulation of the State's monopolistic sectors, to ensure that they do not "fall asleep". China has thus pursued openness audaciously. For example, it is possible to acquire a majority shareholding in many state enterprises, making China more liberal than countries like Japan or Korea. I do not know if you have tried to take majority control of a Japanese or Korea firms, but I believe that many people have tried without much success! Highly protected sectors have also been opened up. For example, in the financial sector, which is not yet completely open, numerous foreign companies and joint ventures have entered the market. Lastly, in sectors that have not yet been opened up officially, such as distribution, various derogations already allow foreign companies to operate. But what is the result?

The result is that whole swathes of Chinese industry are now controlled by foreign firms. This may be seen especially in sectors like mobile telephones, microcomputers and soft drinks, to say nothing of integrated circuit boards.

What can be concluded from this? In his memoirs, Henry Kissinger recounts a very interesting episode. After the death of Mao, he met, within the space of 24 hours, China's leader Hua Guo Feng, who is now forgotten, and Deng Xiaoping. Both of them outlined the future of China, but their visions were radically different. The former envisaged the evolution of the Chinese economy, given the globalisation of production and management techniques, within the framework of central planning. The latter predicted that the market economy would develop considerably. Hypotheses about the future may thus be made, and a question may be asked in conclusion. Is it not possible to believe that two tendencies still coexist in China, even though the principal protagonists have now quit the political scene? The first is a technocratic tendency, and the second a far more market-oriented one. Returning to the examples of the automobile and finance industries, it is striking to note that the first is still characterised by a sort of Plan, whereby there is an attempt to generate a certain number of groups respecting certain criteria, especially relating to production capacity, modernisation, integration, and Chinese techniques. As for the world of finance, it is to be noted that in the insurance industry, a group like AIG has been able to set up a company in Shanghai that is 100% foreign-owned, without any constraints on its activities except those relating to their geographical limits. In this case, the official stance of the authorities is to state that "presently we observe that the Chinese financial sector cannot meet competition with foreign companies, but when they will be able to, we will open the market entirely". Returning to what Zhu Rong Ji replied to a group of Japanese bankers who asked him "when will you open up the Chinese market?" he stated that:

"Gentlemen, if you want the Chinese market to open in the area of financial institutions, then help Chinese financial institutions face competition from global groups. At that point we will open the market."

PART 2

An Insight into Business Opportunities

CHAPTER 7
THE COMPARATIVE PRODUCTIVITY OF SETTING UP IN CHINA:THE EXPERIENCE OF ST MICROELECTRONICS IN THE INDUSTRIAL ZONE NEAR SHENZHEN

Alain DUTHEIL[*]

SGS-Thomson Microelectronics (ST Microelectronics) was created in 1987. The company was borne out of the marriage of two semi-conductor producing companies: Thomson semi-conductor, and the Italian company SGS microelectronica. Semi-conductors are at the heart of electronic systems. They are the brain, the memory and the nervous system.

1. A GLOBAL PRESENCE

ST Microelectronics is present throughout the world. Its turnover was greater than $4 billion in 1996, of which 56% was generated outside Europe, with 27% in the Asia-Pacific region, 6% in Japan, 44% in Europe, and 23% in America. This corresponds to a geographical breakdown into four regions: the Americas, Europe, Asia-Pacific and Japan (see Graph 1).

There are 17 production sites spanning the globe, along with 3 research and development plants. The areas of application are as follows:

1.   Consumer electronics, TV and multimedia;
2.   Information Technology;
3.   Telecommunications;
4.   Automobiles.

The group's 30 major clients are also spread across the globe (see Graph 2), and include the largest companies in the United States, Europe and Japan.

---

[*] Chairman, ST Microelectronics.

Graph 1:

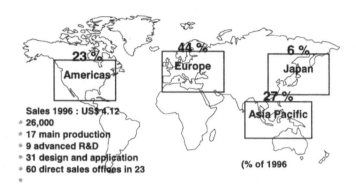

ST. MICROELCTRONICS :
A GLOBAL SEMICONDUCTOR

23 %
Americas

44 %
Europe

6 %
Japan

27 %
Asia Pacific

Sales 1996 : US$ 4.12
* **26,000**
* **17 main production**
* **9 advanced R&D**
* **31 design and application**
* **60 direct sales offices in 23**
*

(% of 1996

Graph 2:

ST. MICROELECTRONICS : DIVERSIFIED CUSTOMER
BASE

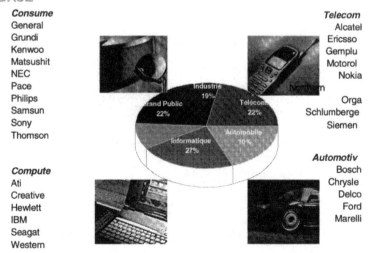

Consume
General
Grundi
Kenwoo
Matsushit
NEC
Pace
Philips
Samsun
Sony
Thomson

Compute
Ati
Creative
Hewlett
IBM
Seagat
Western

Telecom
Alcatel
Ericsso
Gemplu
Motorol
Nokia

Orga
Schlumberge
Siemen

Automotiv
Bosch
Chrysle
Delco
Ford
Marelli

Industri 19%
Grand Public 22%
Telecom 22%
Automobile 10%
Informatique 27%

For a company like ST. Microelectronics, which produces semi-conductors, the main interest of a Chinese presence lies in the national market. The semi-conductor industry is in a market that doubles every five years, equivalent to 15% growth per annum, but characterised by phases of rapid acceleration and brutal regression. In 1996, the market fell by 8%, compared to 30% growth in the previous years. There are many reasons for such growth, one of which is the phenomenon of "penetration". Semi-conductors are being used more and more in electronic systems and their relative share in such systems rose from 4% in 1965 to 19% in 1995. In the year 2000, the global market for semi-conductors should stand at $300 billion – its present value being $140 billion (see Graph 3).

Graph 3:

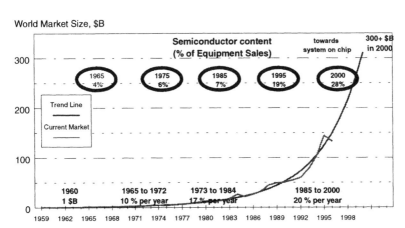

RISING SEMICONDUCTOR CONTENT FUELS DEMAND

Source : WSTS, DATAQUEST, SGS-THOMSON

2. THE REASONS FOR THE EVOLUTION

During the 1960s, the market essentially covered large-scale Information Technology systems and telecommunication infrastructure, representing only about 20% of the mass of the market. These markets were proportional to the economic importance of the regions, that is to say their GNP, whereas today the semi-conductor market is proportional to the industrial dynamism of a region.

In the 1970s and 1980s, the United States essentially held the "leadership" of the market, followed by Japan and Europe. Today, the market is more and more a mass market, with the growing use of IT and electronic systems in consumer goods, via the use of terminals and PCs.

Asia has become one of the most dynamic continents in this field, followed by the United States, Japan and Europe. The market will continue to develop as electronics are flooding consumer goods and invading personal applications such as the mobile phone, the smart card (which is expanding rapidly throughout the world) and the electronic car.

As the market is ever more oriented towards individuals, Asia is becoming more and more important to the semi-conductor industry, and especially China which has well understood what is at stake. The share of high technology in industrial value-added represents about 20% in the United States and Japan, 17% in Europe and 5% in China. But, annual growth in spending on high-technology sectors is rising fastest in China (see Table 1).

Table 1:

MAJOR NATIONS' STRENGTH
IN INFORMATION TECHNOLOGY

	Percentage of High Tech in Industry	Annual Growth Hi Tech investment average % 1987-1994
USA	24%	8.1%
Europe	17%	7.2%
Japan	22%	7.8%
Asia	15%	18%
China	5%	17%

*An intensive effort is being pursued by China
in the use of information technologies*

China has embarked on a massive effort to use information technology, which is why the government supports these technologies and especially the semi-conductor industry.

Concerning the production of electronic goods and China's main product: one billion watches and 280 million calculators are produced in China. The market is thus important today, and can but grow in the years-ahead (Table 2). Chinese output of systems is estimated at $33 billion, equivalent to French output. By 2000, Chinese production will have doubled to $70 billion (see Table 2).

Table 2:

ELECTRONIC GOODS PRODUCTION
(Main products - 1996)

Color TV	21 million
B&W TV	13 million
Recorder	365 million
Disk / CD	80 million
Watch	1030 million
Clocks	186 million
Games	78 million
Calculator	279 million
PC	3 $bn
Telecom	6 $bn

In 1996 production is estimated to be 3 $bn - equivalent to French production (4% of world Production)

Since 1993, yearly growth in China is 26%

In 2000, it is estimated Chinese production will reach 70 $bn (6% of world production)

3. ST. MICROECONOMICS' PLANTS

There are two types of factory in this industry. "Front-End" factories make chips, and there are a number in France, including plants in Tours, Rennes, and in the Aix-en-Provence, with another factory under construction in the latter region. Such plants are substantial investments, costing about $1 billion, and employing between 800 and 900 staff, of which half are technicians and engineers. The work of such plants is highly technical, and requires much know-how.

The criteria for selecting such a site are based firstly on the presence of a local market, clients who need local support, followed by the potential of local engineers and technicians whose presence is vital in assisting clients. Economic considerations include investment aid. Indeed, most countries today compete to attract semi-conductor industries, and so are willing to help semi-conductor producers substantially. Lastly, the presence of know-how, infrastructure and logistics must be taken into account.

"Back-End" plants are the second type. In these, chips are placed in a box which allows clients to test them, integrate them into the products they are making, and lastly use them.

Investment in "Back-End" plants is far more modest, running to around one hundred million dollars. However, such plants employ more personnel, about 1550 people, of which 20% are engineers and technicians with average technical and know-how needs. The know-how required to operate a "Back-End" factory is very easy to transfer from one unit to another. The importance of the market as a criteria for setting up such a factory is less. From an economic point of view, labour costs are the determing factor in location (see Table 3).

Table 3: Manufacturing Facilities in the Semi-Conductor Industry

Features

	Front-End Fabs	Back-End Fabs
Investment	1,000 M$	100 M$
People	800 out of which 50% engineers and technicians	1,500 out of which 20% engineers and technicians
Know-how	Very high	Moderate

Criterias for new Locations

	Font-Ends Fabs	Back-End Fabs
Market	Important	Moderate
Economy	Aid to investment	Cost of labor
Know how	Very important	Low
Infrastructure and Logistics	Important	Important

ST. Microelectronics has "Front-End" factories in Italy, France, the United States and Singapore. "Back-End" plants are set up in locations with low labour costs, but which are still close to large markets. There are plants in the Mediterranean Basin, in Malaysia and in Singapore. The latest is in Shenzhen, north of Hong Kong (see Graph 4).

It is important to note that this latter location is close to those in Malaysia and Singapore, as this allows personnel (who are essentially Chinese, resident and working in Malaysia and Singapore, as well as being Mandarin-speaking), to be seconded to Shenzhen where they have been able to help with the launching of the plant.

The structure of the company is that of a joint venture, 60% controlled by ST. Microelectronics, and 40% controlled by SEG High Tech (i.e. the Shenzhen Electronic Group High Tech, an industrial group whose subsidiary was especially created for this joint venture). SEG High Tech has had the political support of the municipality of Shenzhen and the region, as well as clearly that of the Centre. Any investment in China is not possible without these three conditions being met.

The Board of STS is made up of 7 members: 4 from ST Microlectronics and 3 from SEG. The Chair is held by SGS, while the management of STS is in the hands of ST Microelectronics (see Graph 5).

Graph 5:

ST SHENZHEN

Joint Venture

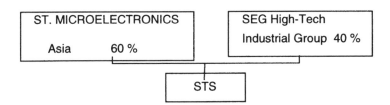

✓ **7 Board Members**
   • **4 ST. MICROELECTRONICS**

  • **3 SEG**
✓ **President: ST. MICROELECTRONICS**
✓ **Management: ST. MICROELECTRONICS**

The Chinese subsidiary was created in December 1994. The construction of the plant, which includes a floor space of 25000m^2, began in January 1995. At the same time, a total of 150 staff from all levels (managers, technicians, operators etc.) were sent for training in Malaysia and Singapore. Some stayed for 6 months, working on production lines similar to those that were being set up in Shenzhen.

The construction of the plant was completed in July 1996, and to industrialists familiar with the field, this is not an unreasonable delay. The first machines were installed a year ago, the time to ensure their correct functioning, so that production began in November 1996. Thus the experience is recent. In order to conclude in 1994, the first discussions with the Chinese partners began in 1991. The expansion of production to capacity levels has occurred relatively rapidly, and is in line with the normal standards of the industry, found in other countries. By the 1st quarter 1997, more than 5 million components had been fabricated, a level expected to double by the 3rd and 4th quarters.

4. PRODUCTIVITY COMPARISONS

Table 4 presents results which allow 3 plants producing the same items to be compared.

Productivity, measured in the number of components/hour, and which depends on the machines and the personnel on the lines, is similar in the plants in Malaysia, Marocco and China.

Table 4:

RESULT

	Casablanca (Morocco)	Muar (Malaysia)	Shenzhen (China)
Productivity Base 100	100	130	114
Industrial Performance	97	95	96
Direct Cost / hour US$	3.60	2.90	1.30
Average indirect cost US$/year	23,100	17,900	20,600

Production returns (i.e. the number of correctly functioning components) are roughly the same everywhere.

Hourly wage costs per operator are between $1.30 in China and $3.6 in Marocco. The various costs linked to transferring the location of production to China are included in this rate. By comparison, labour costs in France are $20, $20 in Italy, and $15-16 in the United States.

Indirect costs (technicians and engineers) fall between $17900 in Malaysia and $23100 in Marocco. Costs fall by half when moving northwards out of Shenzhen, but then infrastructural difficulties arise.

5. CONCLUSION

Performance does not depend on geographic location. The essential factor is the management of a company, as has been shown by the plant in Singapore during the last 25 years. Management methods and the way they are implemented are the keys to the success of setting up a plant in any particular location.

ANNEX

BACKGROUND INFORMATION

Shenzhen Electronics Group (SEG) is a Chinese Company controlled by the local Government of Shenzhen. This broad range electronics Company specialised in exportation runs several commercial and technological activities: computer and telecom products, semiconductor and integrated circuits, import-export, financial and real estate investment management.

Shenzhen High Tech Industrial Group is majority owned by SEG and has been created in view of the collaboration with ST in order to guarantee the success of the joint venture

HISTORY

STS creation	*December 8, 1994*
ST people in training in Malaysia and Singapore (Approx. 150 individual as of today)	*August, 1995*
Building start up	*January, 1995*
End of building up	*July, 1996*

CHAPTER 8
A CONTROLLED TRANSITION OR ANARCHY IN CHINA? THE CASE OF MARITIME TRANSPORT

Eric BOUTEILLER[*]

China's maritime sector is at the heart of the reforms of the 1990s, making it representative of the country's development and internationalisation. It illustrates the main axes of the transition, as well as the scale of the problems faced by the Chinese authorities[1], as far as these can be observed given their relatively opaque environment. The area analysed is principally that of container traffic, which corresponds roughly to international trade in manufactured products.

1. THE PORTS

Chinese maritime transport has experienced remarkable progress, which corresponds to the development of trade and the export industry. Between 1981 and 1996, traffic (in both directions) rose from 100,000 to 8 million Twenty-Foot Equivalents (TFEs)[2]. Volume growth in 1996 alone stood at 20%. This strong progression is the result of two, linked trends: the growth of China's foreign trade, along with the rising containerisation of goods exported from China. It has been accompanied by massive investment to allow specialised ships to be accepted by Chinese ports, the handling of containers, and progressively the establishment of a complete transport system allowing containers to be freighted to the hinterland[3].

At the same time, the institutional framework of the port infrastructure has been transformed gradually. Prior to the reforms, the Ministry of Communications was directly responsible for planning; investment and the day-to-day running of all port infrastructures which were of national importance. As

---

[*] Deputy Director, Eurasia Institute, HEC.
1. This research is the result of several years of study of documents and surveys, on the ground, of the actors involved. Some of the results have been published in the *Journal de la marine marchande*. Hong Kong is not covered in this presentation, as its situation is radically different, even though the influence of the territory on the mainland has rise very rapidly within this sector.
2. A Twenty-Foot Equivalent is the unit of measure relating to containers that are twenty feet long.
3. The convertion of roads bridges and tunnels so that they can cope with the size of container shipments.

of 1983-1984, the Ministry has undergone a vast programme of *xiafang*, that is to say the decentralisation of responsibilities[4]. Following this reorganisation, responsibility for the ports is shared with the municipalities in which they are situated. Daily management is essentially left to local authorities, which usually also includes the nomination of port directors. The Ministry only retains powers to set the guidelines for the sector, as well as approving major investment projects (generally more than $30 million).

In principle, Chinese companies are free to invest in port infrastructures as long as they do not exceed the threshold defined by local authorities. This threshold may be very high, as for example in the case of the China Merchants conglomerate which developed a port with complete autonomy, in the Special Economic Zone of Shenzhen. Furthermore, foreign companies have been progressively allowed to invest in China. Thus, Hong Kong entrepreneur Li Kashing acquired a 51% stake in the container port of Shanghai, which was set up as a company to this end.

The influx of foreign direct investment, along with new competition, has overturned the hierarchy of Chinese ports. Formerly, each national installation handled approximately the same volume of traffic. Henceforth, Shanghai has clearly surged into the lead, attaining 1.97 million TFEs in 1996, more than twice the level of any other port[5]. Qingdao has also significantly profited from this situation, overtaking Tianjin, its "traditional" rival. Lastly, the port of Shenzhen surpassed Canton for the first time in 1996[6].

Qualitatively, the most active ports have also been able to "capture" certain international shipping companies whose vessels stop-off directly in these ports, rather than using Hong Kong as a hub for the south, and (to a lesser extent) Kobe in the north. In the medium term, the supremacy of these two latter centres could be challenged, as the cost of handling containers in China is approximately a third of that in Hong Kong and Kobe[7]. For the moment, however, the competitive position of these two ports continues to be strong, thanks to the quality of their transport systems as well as the vitality of the port communities, which remain without comparison in continental China.

The growing autonomy of the ports has been accompanied by numerous aberrations that have followed the de-structuring of the planning system. Local

---

4. Except for the port of Qinghuangdao, which is specialised in the exportation of coal.
5. Contrary to what is often said, Shanghai remains far behind Hong Kong (whose traffic stood at 13.4 million TFEs in 1996), and does not constitute a viable, economic alternative to the latter because its port is only 10 meters deep, as opposed to more than 14 meters in Hong Kong.
6. See "The Transport of International Containers in China, in 1996" (in Chinese), The Chinese Maritime Affaires Weekly, Beijing, 10 February 1997, pp. 8-10.
7. Kwok Kwok Chuen, "Is Hong Kong losing its trading centre status", Standard Chartered Viewpoints, Hong Kong, August 1996, 6p.

officials have stated that such autonomy is affected by "blind horse" syndrome[8]. The ports of the south no longer provide statistics nor monthly reports to the Ministry of Communications. Competition between ports is fierce, as each is henceforth dependent on its own earnings (taxes on traffic or related activities) to finance operations and investments.

For example, the Province of Hebei and the municipality of Beijing have formed an alliance to develop infrastructure to compete with the port of Tianjin, despite the fact that the two ports are neighbours. Hebei and Beijing would like to benefit from the numerous financial and economic advantages of the port of Tianjin, which the latter's authorities refuse them. Overall, the current disorganisation has led to twice as much handling capacity as there is traffic, according to the Chinese authorities themselves.

2. THE TRANSPORTERS

China's maritime companies have experienced similar change. Prior to reform, the sector was organised on the basis China's territorial administrative structure (centre, provinces, districts etc.), and by mode of transport (river, coastal and long haul transport). The Ministry of Communications retained final, but direct control.

During the first phase of reforms, each level of the administration obtained management control of part of the fleet. Long-haul capacity was drawn together under China Ocean Shipping (Cosco)[9], long-distance river traffic under Changjiang Shipping, while coastal trade was distributed between the coastal provinces. Since 1984, the monopolies of these various entities have been abolished. The transport companies have thus faced head-on competition during the 1990s, compared with the marginal competition of the 1980s. In 1997, this competition has been very strong in coastal traffic and for small shipments, but has remained relatively limited for long haul traffic, given the scale of the investments involved, which are beyond the means of most provinces and municipalities. Only the former State Brokerage Agency for Transport and Transit Trade has been able to develop a long haul fleet, and so take part of Cosco's activity. The directors of the Ministry of Communications speak of a period of a "Hundred Flowers", as China now has 370 officially registered, maritime transport companies, compared to only 10 in 1978.

Numerous difficulties have arisen in the domestic market because of the incomplete economic transition. According to China's economic actors themselves, there are problems of systematic dumping, strong market opacity,

---

8. Xiao Zhongxi, "The reinforcement of controls on construction in container ports is necessary" (in Chinese), Communication and Transport, Beijing, 27 January 1997, p.5.
9.»The Cosco group conquering the world" (in Chinese), Report for the 35th anniversary of Cosco, Beijing, April 1996, 10p.

the non-adherence to safety norms along with significant fraud (the siphoning-off of material etc.). Theft of coal by pirate gangs is a daily occurrence on China's major river axis, the Changjiang. Even long haul transport, which is relatively sheltered given the importance of the investments required, is affected. Some provinces have developed their own fleets and have tried to capture the traffic of companies situated on their territory using various non-economic means (such as administrative orders and other forms of pressure). The forces released by the reforms have also affected the structure of Cosco. The long haul fleet has been split-up into 5 regional groups which have also manifested a striving for autonomy. For example, the use of a Canton-managed ship by the general directorate of the company required an agreement with the local administration.

As of 1992, a certain taking charge and deepening of reforms has been discernible. On the one hand, administrative authority over Cosco has been clarified: subsidies from the Ministry have been transformed into "political credits". But Cosco has obtained greater financial autonomy. Container leasing activities were grouped together and quoted on the Hong Kong stock exchange, under the name of Cosco Pacific. Cosco thus has a strong, autonomous financial arm which has allowed it to regroup its shareholdings in container terminals in China, and, in the future, set up an offensive acquisition strategy in the Far East[10].

At the same time, internal company «baronies» have been partially dismembered through the centralised management of the fleet, and then the centralised finance of companies. Such strengthening of control deepened as of 1995, with the restructuring of the company, and has been carried out by reducing staffing "beginning at the top". In a year, the general management of the company lost a third of its directors (though maintaining its activity). These individuals were dispatched to the subsidiaries of the group. This has allowed wage scales to be made more flexible, with the salaries of key managers increasing substantially. The reform has not yet been applied to the rest of the organisation, because of the impossibility of resorting to redundancies and due to a lack of finance.

The reorganisation of Cosco's management system indicates the new orientation taken by the economic reforms since 1995-1996. By Chinese standards, Cosco's financial situation is relatively sound, as it has access to the international market and so has earnings in dollars. The situation is completely different for a river shipping company, like Changjiang Shipping for example, which according to its directors would like to shift from having 120,000 employees to 20,000, without impacting on its activity levels.

---

10. Tracy Woo, "Cosco Pacific", report by BNP Primeast, Hong Kong, June 1997, 18p.

The strategic conditions facing Chinese companies have been profoundly modified by the rise of foreign competition. The gradual opening of markets adopted by Beijing had made it possible to delay the impact of foreign competition, but now such competition has become head-on. Foreign transport companies were allowed to set up representative offices in 1992. But it was only in 1995 that they were permitted to sell their services in China, though they must pass via a State maritime agency and a series of public bodies to negotiate freight and credit conditions. Nevertheless, the shock to Chinese shippers has been great. Within a year, the share of China's foreign trade shipped by Chinese companies has fallen from 70% to 30%.

It seems that the decision taken in 1996 by the Chinese authorities to create a "freight exchange" in Shanghai[11] consists of reducing the impact on Chinese shippers of the opening of the market to foreign competition[12]. The official objective is to organise the entire market, by forcing all Chinese and foreign actors to declare the terms of their contracts, so that the competition is more transparent. But, according to international shippers and loaders, the measure is designed to control and distort competition in favour of Chinese shippers. China is the only country to adopt such measures.

3. THE OUTLOOK

Fundamentally, the transition of maritime transport has drawn on "anarchy", through the decentralisation of decision-making without the creation of a new reference framework. This strategy is deliberate, aimed at dismantling the former planning system. The creation of a system of integration rules (between the ports and the companies) has only just begun, and will take time. The authorities are perplexed, as they have observed the major role played by market forces, but do not want to let these express themselves fully because of political reasons. Recourse to unemployment and privatisation are ideological taboos, even if current experiments are generally conducted along these lines.

Another constraint by Beijing on this "anarchy" stems from China's national ambitions, which cannot be doubted. China wants to have one of the world's primary maritime transport capacities, and the experience of the Newly Industrialised Countries in Asia demonstrates that this is possible while export industry expands.

The "controlled anarchy" practised by Beijing is becoming more and more fragile, because of market forces and the centrifugal tensions reigning in China. The absence of a true, national development policy for maritime transport in China is an example of this. The central and local authorities are not

---

11. The Shanghai Shipping Exchange.
12. See, for example, the presentation by Mr Pierre Harent, Director CMA, Equiport, Le Havre, May 1997.

able to reach agreement in the selection of hubs for the Chinese network. The Ministry of Communications takes refuge in such "strategic ambiguity", by designating zones and not ports. Ultimately, China will have three basic hubs:
- Hong Kong and Shenzhen for the south;
- Shanghai and Beilun for the east, and
- Tianjin, Qindao and Dalian for the north.

Yet within each region competition among the ports is ferocious, and the ports employ all non-economic means available to capture traffic from their neighbours. The shippers face a similar problem, even if the intensity is less in the sector which is massively dominated by Cosco. Unable to ensure that the rules of the game are fair, Beijing has become a spectator of the competition, intervening only to ensure that the national interest is respected.

CHAPTER 9

THE EVOLUTION OF CHINA AS SEEN BY A LARGE FRENCH UTILITY: THE EXEMPLE OF THE ELECTRICITY SECTOR

Vincent de RIVAZ[*]

1. THE GLOBAL SITUATION OF THE WORLD ELECTRICITY MARKET

The situation of the world electricity market is presently characterised by the very rapid recomposition of the large electricity systems. For the sake of privatisation, the existing systems have been "de-integrated", so that they can be more easily sold off "in apartments". Private capital has been called upon to carry out new works, a concept known as that of Independent Private Producers (IPP).

All this is taking place in countries in which growth is low (as in Europe) through the recomposition of existing systems, through the change of ownership and shareholding and in countries with strong growth (as in Latin America and Asia). The stakes are considerable, with hundreds of billions of francs being invested in the global electricity sector each year, by new actors.

2. THE REASONS FOR EDF'S INTERNATIONALISATION

In a few years, some larger leaders will have acquired key positions in this market. EDF's strategic decision has been simple. Given the alternative of being a spectator or an actor, the company has decided to be an actor, so as to reinforce its global competitiveness by investing in these operations, as an investment operator. This means carrying out its basic functions in production, transportation and the distribution of electricity, so as to master its own investment risks and reap the expected benefits.

[*] Executive Vice-President, International Division, EDF.

A few key statistics: in France, EDF has approximately a capacity of one hundred thousand Megawatts (MGW), serving about 30 million customers. Its goal is to generate a third of its turnover abroad, within the next ten years, half-coming from production, half from distribution. In other words, EDF seeks to control the supply of between 20000 and 30000 MGW outside France, serving 15 to 20 million customers (the figures inside France being 100000 MGW and 30 million respectively).

3. THE PLACE OF CHINA IN EDF'S STRATEGY

China figures strongly within these objectives, especially in the area of production. We believe that to fulfil our objectives we have to produce an extra 3000 MGW per year abroad, of which a third (i.e. 1000 MGW) should come from China, a country that requires an annual increase in capacity of 15000 MGW, with 20% drawing on foreign capital. If our objective is reached it will constitute a quarter of the Chinese market, open to foreign investors. This is a major challenge for EDF.

EDF's involvement in China is not recent, and goes back about 15 years. The first phase was very clearly one in which trade and co-operation were carried out in the technical field, be it in nuclear, hydraulic or thermal production; the design and execution of transport and distribution facilities; in laboratories; and with respect to pricing and planning.

The second phase occurred during the second half of the 1980s, once China had undertaken some strategic thinking about the evolution of the organisation of its electricity sector. In 1987 a very high-level delegation from the Ministry of Energy visited a number of European countries to see how the various models of the electricity industry were developing.

The "Socialist Market Economy" found EDF to be a high-performance and competitive enterprise. It's industrial, financial and management results were considered as positive. However, the Chinese were also interested to find such results within a State-Owned Enterprise, guaranteeing a public service and belonging 100% to a single shareholder, yet nevertheless developing within a market economy.

This fed the second phase of co-operation between EDF and the Chinese which, after the laying of technical foundations, concentrated on training, and exchanges in the field of company management. From the beginning of the 1990s up until now, EDF has received about sixty leading officials from China's electricity sector, who have spent several weeks with EDF in order to be trained in the management methods of our company. This should continue.

The third phase consists of becoming an investor in China. The two first phases allowed EDF to acquire the assets needed for the success of the third phase.

The largest joint–venture investment carried out in China's electricity sector was concluded by a consortium in which EDF was associated as the foreign partner, along with colleagues in Hong Kong, and the electricity company of the Province of Shandong as the Chinese partner. The two stages of this project will yield 3000 MGW, representing an investment for EDF of about FF700 million, over a number of years.

Almost at the same time, EDF (as part of a 100% foreign consortium) obtained the first BOT (Build Operate Transfer) concessionary contract in the Province of Ghangxi, in the face of tough international competition. The decision to undertake an entirely foreign BOT was made by the SPC (the State Planning Commission), and did not appeal much to the Ministry of Energy. However, the SPC wanted to carry out such a test in a province that is not very attractive to foreign capital.

The law should intervene in this field. It is a provincial project, and hence a provincial risk, but the comfort letter of the SPC, which commits itself to ensuring that the engagements of the Province are respected, provides the project with official support from the Centre.

In parallel to these major operations, significant investments in the nuclear energy field are being undertaken in China. In this area, EDF is running up against the problems of centralisation and decentralisation.

The first French success in the nuclear field was recorded in 1986 (with the signing of a contract for the construction of the Nuclear Power Station of Daya Bay, in Guandong), and especially the coming on-line of the power station in 1995. In 1995, EDG signed two new *tranches*, in the proximity of Lingao. This constitutes the beginning of a nuclear "programme".

At the same time, the Chinese have launched other experiences with the Russians and the Canadians in the area of heavy water. The Chinese are currently in an experimental phase, seeking to make a strategic choice at the turn of the century: the technological choice of the "Chinese industry" will in the end be Chinese, but will be the fruit of technology brought in from abroad, necessitating the choice of a foreign partner.

At present, EDF has to manage this opportunity with the desire of becoming China's partner. The long-term objective is to base such activity locally, and to make China independent in nuclear energy, which appears as the only means of managing nuclear security. If the Chinese do not master nuclear energy, they will not be able to master security. All this is taking place between the Province of Guandong and the Centre, the decision to develop a nuclear energy industry being political.

To be sure, the decisions of Guandong were made in accordance with the Centre in 1985 and 1995, and especially with the support of Li Peng. As for the following phase, which includes the location policy of the nuclear energy industry, and given the stakes involved, the decision must clearly be taken by the Centre.

EDF must find a way of consolidating its relations with the local client and with the other provinces, without giving the impression to the Centre that it is favouring any particular province.

As in China's other sectors, the electricity industry is evolving. To us, this evolution seems to be very well thought-out, methodical and constant. Despite a certain number of hesitations, divisions and contradictions, its orientation is understood and known.

The former bureaucracies which managed the electricity sector have to become companies. Economic realities must prevail, especially with respect to prices. The provinces have to be able to take charge of a certain number of decisions. A striking example of this long and controlled evolution is the creation of a national electricity company (the State Power Company), which is managed by the same individuals who manage the Ministry of Energy that the company is meant to replace. Hence, there is no abrupt break, as the individuals in charge are the same. Nevertheless, real reform is being undertaken.

The evolution is being carried out with a rationalisation, a separation of official and corporate responsibility, the creation of a regulating function at the Centre and the strong decentralisation of operational decisions. All together, this will be one of the motives for the development of the Chinese electricity industry, which has a key role to play in the development of the Chinese economy.

With a production objective of an additional 15000 MGW per annum, the Chinese have revealed the scale of their needs. Yet even if these targets are reached, they will probably not meet all needs.

For EDF, which has been involved in China over the last 15 years, the investments undertaken so far are investments for 20 years. It is thus too early to reach an assessment. However, the success of EDF operations in China, in the face of the challenges of the 21st Century, will shape the overall image of EDF in the future.

CHAPTER 10
THE ATTRACTIVENESS OF CHINA TO FOREIGN INVESTORS

Samuel PINTO[*]

Investing in China is clearly an act of faith, as the country does not exhibit great economic transparency. Its economic statistics generate controversy, but the economy is very powerful and is growing very rapidly. Financiers can also be most reassured by foreign direct investment (FDI) in China: $40 billion have flowed in each year, during the last three years, proving the health of the Chinese economy. China is also known to have very large reserves. As a result, China will be a larger economic power in the medium term. Some figures are already very revealing: 75% of all toys sold in the United States are made in China, and the Chinese world (including Taiwan and Hong Kong) controls nearly a quarter of the world's foreign currency reserves.

1. THE SHORT TERM ECONOMIC CYCLE

Economic growth slowed down abruptly in 1995, and even more so in 1996 and 1997. The domestic economy is still performing slowly, as witnessed by the extremely slow rise in imports. When an economy's imports are practically flat, it proves that demand growth is very weak. Exports, however, have risen rapidly, so that the trade balances chalk–up an extraordinary performance in 1997. The economy is thus outward-looking, extrovert, but restrained by being at then end of a downward cycle which started in 1993 with the application of a restrictive policy aimed at reducing overheating which had seen inflation rise to 25%. From this point of view, it is important to note that liquidity is favourable in the financial market. Indeed, inflation is very low: probably less than 3% in 1997. The growth of credit is running at about 20% in nominal terms, thus in the order of 20% in real terms. Under these conditions much money is available, which is not being invested in the real economy because of sluggish growth, and which is thus moving into the financial markets.

Lastly, China is clearly liberalising rapidly, via privatisation and the convertibility of its currency, which has been stable over the last 2 to 3 years. Privatisations are being carried out by the injection of assets into companies listed in Hong Kong, by the development of mergers and acquisitions, and lastly

---

[*] Director at the Compagnie Financière Edmond de Rothschild Banque.

thanks to developments relating to the treatment of minority shareholders. It should also be noted that the Chinese financial market is liberalising rapidly.

2. BASIC INDICATORS OF THE SIZE OF THE CHINESE FINANCIAL MARKET

The economy is now capitalist, and has a financial market that is becoming very important. About 700 companies are quoted. In May 1997, 4 companies were brought into the market each week. The total stock market value stands at around $250 billion. The Hong Kong market's value is about $450 billion, and France's more or less twice this. Daily trading volume in the Chinese exchanges exceeds $2 billion, about the same as the Paris Bourse. While there were no markets a few years ago, today the Chinese markets have become more sophisticated, and in any case larger.

Several types of stock exist:

- So-called H stocks of Chinese companies quoted in Hong Kong;
- B stocks of Chinese companies quoted in China (in Shanghai and Shenzhen), which are in principle reserved for foreigners;
- N stocks, quoted in New York;
- Redships, which are stocks for Chinese companies quoted in Hong Kong and whose head-quarters are also registered in Hong Kong (usually owned by Chinese interests);
- A stocks, which are the most important, are stocks of Chinese quoted companies which may only be bought by domestic investors. Daily trading in such stocks runs at $2 billion, and the market capitalisation stands at nearly $200 billion.

The extraordinary development of these markets has led to a strong rise in stock prices over the last year, notably as the index of so-called redship stocks (of Chinese companies quoted in Hong Kong) has practically tripled since 1996, rising by nearly 70% since the beginning of 1997. The increases have been less spectacular for other stocks that foreigners can buy: H and B stocks have been rising more or less in line with the Hong Kong index and international stock markets, which have been euphoric since mid 1996 and have shown it. It is normal enough that such stocks rise, given the economic cycle, and because more and more companies are being quoted. Of the companies quoted in China, there is a strong concentration in Shanghai (117 companies), and Guandong (39). However, companies are quoted throughout the country, even in China's most isolated provinces, which proves the truly spectacular nature of stock market development. Furthermore, the companies that have been authorised to go public during the next months, and in the coming years, are more in the centre of the country, rather than in the coastal zones where many are already quoted. Furthermore, the Chinese government would like to double the programme of quotations in the market for stocks, reserved for the Chinese, in order to dampen strong speculation.

3. How to Invest in China?

Many investment funds are interested in China, and have invested about $7 billion. They are located either in Hong Kong, or in other countries specialised in China, excluding of course investment funds that are mainly interested in all of Asia and especially in China (generally more than 50%). The formidable development of the Chinese stock markets has generated a large supply of stocks, whose market value will reach $10 billion in 1997, as opposed to less than half this figure last year ($5 billion), and only one or two billion in the preceding years. The stock market is growing extremely quickly, probably even more quickly now that the Chinese government has decided to accelerate its development.

The stock market is liquid. Taking A stocks, which are reserved for Chinese, its transaction volumes have reached the levels of the Hong Kong exchange, despite the fact that this market was only established in 1992, and that the Hong Kong market is several decades older and is highly sophisticated.

This rapid development of Chinese stock markets is only beginning. Stock market capitalisation in China is only equivalent to 18% of GNP, compared with 300% in Hong Kong and Malaysia, and 100% of GNP in the United States. France's capitalisation runs at between 30 and 40% of GNP, but many companies in France are not quoted, especially in the public sector. The 18% level in China should develop rapidly in the years ahead.

4. The Rise of The Various Stock Indexes For Exchanges Open to Foreigners

H stocks are issued for large Chinese companies quoted in Hong Kong: these are generally stocks of industrial companies, in the leading sectors of the Chinese economy. Their value has risen, though moderately over the last two or three years, and their level is more or less stable. By looking at companies issuing these stocks, or at those issuing B stocks, it is possible to have a more concrete and especially microeconomic vision of the economic slowdown China experienced in 1995 and 1996, during which stock values hardly progressed at all, while even falling in 1995. The results of publicly quoted Chinese companies were catastrophic during these two years, with sharp falls in profits indicating to what extent the economic situation was worse than the outside world was led to believe. It is hard to believe that growth in 1995 and 1996 was running at 10%, and in any case companies suffered terribly during these two years.

5. THE PERFORMANCE OF REDSHIPS IN HONG KONG

These are companies which usually depend on provinces and cities like Beijing or Shanghai, which are subject to Hong Kong law, and are quoted there. This is the method China has adopted for its privatisation. China has decided not to develop a single stock market, but several, in Shanghai, Shenzhen, and Hong Kong, with companies also being quoted in Singapore and New York. Privatisations with stocks reserved for foreigners are essentially carried out in Hong Kong: these are often companies with no activity to begin with, in which substantial assets are subsequently injected.   A recent example is Shanghai Industrial, the company in charge of developing Shanghai's periphery. A major part of its capital was injected into a company quoted in Hong Kong, which has since become a very important conglomerate.   This is how China privatises, and privatises quickly.

PART 3

China – Hong Kong – Taiwan: The Future of a Triangular Relationship

CHAPTER 11
THE NEW CHINESE NATIONALISM AND ITS INTERNATIONAL CONSEQUENCES

Jean-Luc DOMENACH[*]

PRELIMINARY REMARKS

Much is currently being said about the rise of Chinese nationalism, especially in connection with the return of Hong Kong and the recent, predictable offensives against Taiwan. However, Chinese nationalism is not a new phenomenon. It constitutes a deep undercurrent that was generated by Western Imperialism in the 19th Century, and from which communism itself sprang. More recent events have also flowed from this current, and will continue to do so in the future: the return of Hong Kong a few days ago, that of Macao in 1999, and the offensive against Taiwan. There is thus a long run nationalism, which is completely different to that referred to in press at the moment. The present events in Hong Kong are one of the final chapters in a great cycle of nationalism which began more that a century ago when China entered the modern age through two doors: the first being that of humiliation, and the second that of nationalism.

When communism came to power after 1949, though it was propelled by a deep undercurrent of nationalism as well as by a national war, nationalism was eclipsed, which was both paradoxical and unexpected. The international manifestations of Chinese communism were far more internationalist than they were nationalist. First, it followed the Soviet alliance, before adopting more isolated, anti-imperialist behaviour. In fact, this amounted to a sort of revolutionary universalism, rather than a form of nationalism as strictly defined. Chinese nationalism essentially took refuge in a sort of precautionary behaviour with respect to the country's borders. It was a form of frontier nationalism that led China from the simple alliance with the Soviet Union to intervention in Korea (China was threatened), as well as in Indochina. Generally speaking, nationalism played a relatively limited role in Maoist China, at least as far as the outside world was concerned. Chinese nationalism seemed to withdraw and identify itself with domestic politics. It became a vector in internal transformations. It led to the successive elimination of foreign companies and

---

[*] Scientific Director, Fondation Nationale des Sciences Politiques.

nationals who had remained in China in the early 1950s, and then to the social transformation which was conducted with increasing vigour as of the mid-1950s. Lastly, this form of nationalism motivated the advance of the Maoist Utopia, in which the Chinese people, because they are Chinese and hence white and poor ("Yi qiong er bai"), would ensure its internal transformation, better and to a greater extent than others.

This form of nationalism under Mao Zedong was scarcely modified by Deng Xiaoping.   Indeed, Deng, as Mao, fostered an universalist rather than nationalist foreign policy.   There were some nationalist actions, such as the border war with Vietnam in early 1979.   But, Deng, by favouring the modernisation of the Chinese economy, reinvested the universalism that had been communist with a sort of mercantile universalism.   China had to be open to the world, to trade with it and to receive investment.   This universalism had extremely nationalist origins, and was led by one of China's most nationalist leaders, yet had a relatively restrained foreign impact.   It was British clumsiness when they opened the negotiations over the future of Hong Kong which led Deng Xiaoping to jump on the Hong Kong objective.   In contrast, and again as had been the case under Mao Zedong, nationalism was revived internally, within the framework of internal construction, for national motives.   Deng established and defined a new policy of modernisation as of 1974-75, and began applying it in 1978-79.   This was based on a very strong conception of the Chinese nation, which was to join the most advanced countries of the world.   But this nationalism was different from Mao's, which was utopian and nationalist, whereas Deng's was realist.   Mao's nationalism was generous to a fault; Deng's cynical, but founded on reality, and led Chinese economic policy towards the success we all know today.

1. THE NEW FACTORS IN THE EVOLUTION OF CHINESE NATIONALISM

The first set of factors explains the greater importance of nationalism in domestic politics.   Since the late 1980s, when Deng's policy ran into grave difficulties, the issue of nationalism has been put differently.   Indeed, since this time, domestic politics has no longer been able to satisfy itself with the relatively simple conjunction of the communist impulse and the nationalist impulse. Ideological uncertainty is in the process of marking domestic politics, to a large extent because of the successes of the modernisation policy which has transformed society, has individualised life, sharpened social categories and differentiated regions.   All this together requires an ideological foundation which communism can no longer provide.   It must thus be asked if nationalism will not be used in support of the communist ideology, even more so than was previously the case.   The succession crisis brought on by Deng's death may lead to politicians upping the ante in this field.

A second set of factors stems from China's foreign relations. These are above all linked to the end of the Cold War. The end of the Cold War had led to a situation in which power counts for more than sense, in which this power is more economic than military, and in which the economic performance of countries is decisive in fixing their ranking. China is henceforth faced with an international problem that is far more difficult to manage than before, namely the United States. While the world was divided into two, China (as to a lesser extent France) was able to sell its adhesion to one superpower or another at a very high price, or at least try to give itself the impression of manoeuvring between the two. Now, the situation is far more difficult for a country as ambitious as China. The United States is the sole superpower, and as any superpower, is led inevitably to involving itself in the ideology of others because of its own pretensions, its domestic concerns or in response to public opinion. For China, this is a difficult situation, which is rendered all the more complicated given that its own ideology is in a state of flux, as China must contend not just with a form of American dominance at an economic level, but also with the threat of ideological dominance.

A third set of factors is of a regional nature. The regionalisation of Asia has highlighted two stimulants of nationalism. The first is the ideology of this regionalism, which is based on the ideology of Asian values. This ideology is founded on Confucianism and Islam. The examples of the successes of Singapore and Malaysia, which have both employed this ideology domestically and used it as an instrument in international relations, may inspire China. Another temptation follows naturally from the problem of hegemony which clearly faces all of Asia. This problem goes beyond politics and strategy, and concerns economics as well.

Altogether, China is faced with the issue of deciding to what extent and in which language it is going to seize the opportunity of asserting itself more strongly as a "nation".

2. SIGNS OF THE NEW NATIONALISM

What are the internal and external signs of this new nationalism?

Domestically, Confucianism and official moralism are promoted generally, and reinforced in certain areas, when there is a need for legitimacy. Confucius is celebrated in every way imaginable, though this celebration is limited, as a strict adherence to Confucianism would mean obeying all his precepts and morals. China's past is currently being exalted, including certain episodes of xenophobia or when China was the victim of foreign power. For example, a few episodes of the Opium Wars, which were favourable to China from a military or moral point of view, are presently being celebrated in

Guangdong. A film on the Opium Wars has recently been released, which is a blockbuster and focuses on nationalism. All foreigners living on the continent have observed a complex but real rise in xenophobic sentiment.

Externally, it is the tone adopted by China's foreign policy and diplomacy which is significant. There are some cases of strong xenophobia, and strange episodes, such as the press conferences held by the spokesperson for the Ministry of Foreign Affairs that are, at least in principle, now held in Chinese. The manner in which Beijing negotiated the return of Hong Kong also bears witness to something that goes beyond a rational management of the matter. There is without doubt a desire to demonstrate to the Chinese population that one is a good nationalist. The management of the tensions with Taiwan was clearly troubled both by surges of passion or by a passion to manipulate nationalism, and by the desire of Mr Jiang Zemin to show himself in military uniform. In contrast, the contents of this policy has remained modest. Commentators who complain of the rise of Chinese nationalism are unable to quote many concrete examples bearing out their case, which are not rhetorical, a matter of presentation, or linked to the treatment of foreigners. The only exception concerns the South China Sea. While our Chinese friends have trouble understanding us on this issue, their territorial claims (which stretch down to Indonesia) appear somewhat unrealistic to any foreigner who studies a map of the area. This is all the more unusual given that Chinese diplomacy has on several occasions demonstrated that it is not ignorant of the possibilities of managing this issue through economic co-operation, and through the sharing of responsibilities.

In its international affairs, China appears even more modest than most Third World states. China continues to sign international agreements, such as the international accord on economic and social rights. Its previous refusal to sign such agreements was not motivated by nationalism, but rather by its communist ideology.

The rise of Chinese nationalism is thus a limited phenomenon. This is so firstly because real anxieties concerning China's social and political situation are compensated for by a regular rise in living standards, for most people. People are occupied by things other than politics. Secondly, the crisis following Deng's death, that could have led to a surge in nationalism, was very intelligently delayed by China's leaders. Due to Hong Kong, they decided to close ranks, thus putting aside any escalation of nationalist fever for the time being. Experience (in this case, the time Deng Xiaoping won holding of "possible crises") shows that winning time is always useful. Thirdly, the international environment in trade is not unfavourable to China, whatever its leaders may say. Markets are not systematically closed to its exports, and it cannot be said that China is as disadvantaged by its global and regional environment during the 1990s, as it was during the 1930s. Lastly, Asia's economic performance is generally rather good, and it would be strange to make war in the region, rather than do business. This does not mean that war may never occur in the future, but for the present peaceful occupations dominate. It should also noted that the other countries in Asia are unable of uniting against China (especially with respect to the South China Sea) while the latter is following in their footsteps.

Nevertheless, these limits are not eternal. The performance of the world and regional economies, the manner in which the Chinese leaders will be capable of managing their inevitable power struggles, along with a host of other factors will play a considerable role in the evolution, and perhaps a future rise of Chinese nationalist sentiment. But its importance should not be exaggerated.

CHAPTER 12
THE LONG-TERM CONSEQUENCES OF THE RE-INTEGRATION OF HONG KONG INTO CHINA ON ITS DEVELOPMENT

Georges LEUNG[*]

Five days from now China will resume the exercise of sovereignty over Hong Kong. Under the principle of "one country, two systems", Hong Kong will be managed as a Special Administrative Region of the People's Republic of China. It will be empowered with a high degree of autonomy. Its current administrative, legislative and judiciary systems will continue for 50 years. And its status as an international financial centre will be maintained. In addition, the SAR Government will formulate its own monetary and fiscal policies, independent from those of the central government.

On the economic front, the process of integration with the Mainland started almost two decades ago when China adopted an "open door" policy in late 1978. Hong Kong manufacturers seized the opportunity offered by China's determination to open up and reform its economy. Gradually their operations were shifted to the mainland, particularly the Pearl River Delta region. This relocation of manufacturing and processing to southern China enabled Hong Kong firms to access abundant land and labour resources across the border, and allowed them to remain competitive in the world market.

Hong Kong-controlled production has expanded rapidly in the Mainland, with the associated increase in trade flow fostering the growth of trade-related services in the territory. At the same time, labour released from the local manufacturing sector has been made available for the higher value-added service sector. The result: thereby hastening the transformation of Hong Kong from a manufacturing base to a modern regional business hub.

---

[*] Economic Advisor, Hong Kong and Shanghai Bank.

1. THE SERVICE SECTOR

Hong Kong's economy has advanced to a tertiary production-based structure. Today, the service sector accounts for more than 80% of the territory's gross domestic product, versus 67.5% in 1980. At the same time, the combined share of various industrial sectors—-including manufacturing, construction and utilities— has dwindled from 31.7% to 16.4%.

The economic transformation has also had a noticeable impact on the development of Hong Kong's external trade. Between 1981 and 1995, exports of services rose by an average of 16.5% per annum, against 8.5% for domestic exports and 14.7% for nominal GDP.   In 1994, the value of service exports surpassed that of domestic exports for the first time and was equivalent to 24.0% of the territory's GDP, compared to 20.6% in 1980. Moreover, trade in services has consistently contributed to Hong Kong's overall external balances.   The surpluses have more than offset merchandise deficits in 12 of the past 15 years.

Between 1991 and 1994, large-scale migration of labour from manufacturing to servicing took place. Employment in manufacturing dropped sharply by 40.9%. But over the period, Hong Kong's economy benefited from the service sector's rapid expansion as a result of both increased input and rising labour productivity.

With Hong Kong's economy now owing more than 80% of its production to service industries, there is limited scope for further migration of manufacturing labour into servicing. Manufacturing workers now represent only slightly more than 10% of the local labour force. On the other hand, it will be difficult for the service sector to replicate the achievement of the manufacturing sector in relocating its operations outside Hong-Kong. Additionally, the scope for improvement from capital investment is limited due to the high labour content inherent in many service industries. Some, by their nature, offer little opportunity for gain in productivity.

2. GROWTH AND INFLATION

One benefit of the more service-oriented structure is its relatively stable growth pattern. Economic growth varied widely in the 1980s. It ranged from a low of 0.4% in 1985 to 13.0% in 1987.   The huge swing reflecting the vulnerability of the domestic economy to external shocks. With its development into a service-oriented structure, the economy is now less externally dependent than before. It is likely, therefore, that Hong Kong's economic growth rate will deviate less in the future from its long-term trend rate.   Nevertheless, the economic cycle remains closely related to the performance of the region as a whole. And, in particular, to the performance of Mainland China's economy.

In the past, the relocation of Hong Kong's manufacturing base to the Mainland——to make use of the cheaper human and land resources there— helped to keep the territory's export prices low, despite rising costs in the domestic sector. It was also the cause, however, of the inflationary spiral in Hong Kong. The economy's adjustment mechanism was disabled by the detachment of the normal linkage between price and output. Without relocation, rising inflation would have resulted in higher export prices, which would have cut into the territory's external competitiveness. The consequent slow-down in external trade would have reduced growth and thereby moderated domestic price pressures.

The territory's increasing reliance on services will reactivate the adjustment mechanism.   Relocation on a similar scale to that in the manufacturing sector appears unlikely to be feasible in the service sector, at least in the next few years. Any over-stretched expansion of the service sector would cause a rise in service prices in the form of higher rentals and wages. This would weaken the SAR's external competitiveness and result in a slow-down in the territory's economic growth. Consequently, inflation would moderate to a level low enough to regain competitiveness.

3. CYCLE AND STRUCTURE

Another consequence of Hong Kong's economic integration with the Mainland is on its growth cycle and structure. Deepening economic ties between China and the territory have in the past provided both economies with strong impetus for growth.   The reason: they rely upon each other's comparative advantage to promote their own development.   Hong Kong, as a regional financial centre and a world-class service hub, provides the Mainland with much-needed capital and manufacturing-related support services, while China's abundant land and labour resources strengthen the territory's cost-competitiveness.

China has enjoyed rapid growth since economic reform began in the late 1970s, with real GDP increasing at an average of 10% a year. At the same time, Hong Kong's per capita GDP surpassed the level seen in some major industrial countries.   The closer economic relationship is duly reflected in the increasing correlation of China and the territory's respective economic fortunes. Since the early 1980s, Hong Kong's GDP growth has moved in tandem with the economic cycle in the Mainland.   Such interdependence partly explains the slow-down in Hong Kong's economic growth during 1994 and 1995, after China applied the brakes to cool down its overheated economy.

With the territory now deriving most of its output from the service sector, some may suggest that the growth of Hong Kong's economy has reached a point where new direction is required.   Admittedly, Hong Kong's service sector accounts for more than 80% of its GDP, with a corresponding decline in the contribution from the "domestic" manufacturing sector.   Despite the rapid advancement involved in becoming a major servicing hub in the region, Hong Kong has actually continued to keep a strong link with manufacturing.

With Hong Kong manufacturers having invested heavily in southern China, the territory's manufacturing capabilities have noticeably increased as a result.   The relocation of a production base outside Hong Kong's boundary should not be viewed as a total displacement of the territory's manufacturing industry.   It should be noted, however, that Hong Kong's economic boundary is less well defined than its physical one.   In particular when its role is as a business hub for China, rather than a small and self-contained economy as in the past. There is no doubt that a blurred economic structure will emerge as the territory's economy becomes increasingly intermingled with that of the Mainland.

4. CONCLUSION

In concluding, let me say that the increased importance of the service sector in Hong Kong has brought both opportunities and challenges to the local economy.   Hong Kong's achievement in surpassing the per capita income of some of the industrialised nations is to be applauded.   However, the advancement to a service-oriented structure also implies a slower pace of economic expansion in the future.   But the ability of the local economy to stay competitive as a service-oriented structure will be of great importance.   Particularly, as significant productivity gains become increasingly difficult to attain because of the inherent nature of service provision and the limited feasibility of relocating operations to low-cost areas.   Future growth will rely upon further productivity enhancement.

Fortunately, backed by the rapidly expanding economy in China, where nominal GDP is expected to double in the decade to 2010, the Hong Kong SAR will derive its growth impetus from strengthening its role in facilitating China's economic development through the provision of high-quality services.   Because of the SAR's unique attributes, its comparative advantage in performing such a role is presently unmatched by any other city in China.

Closer economic integration with the Mainland will translate into Hong Kong developing further as a cosmopolitan type of economy.   Its focus will be on its role as mainly a financial and servicing centre.   Financial integration with the mainland system will most likely take place in conjunction with China gradually opening up its financial sector in the coming decades.   As the territory's existing economic system will remain for another 50 years after 1997, its economic structure will amalgamate with the much bigger Chinese economy in order to continue to prosper.   And I have full confidence that Hong Kong's best days lie ahead.

CHAPTER 13
ECONOMIC RELATIONS BETWEEN CHINA, TAIWAN AND HONG KONG[*]

HEH-SONG WANG[*]

On July 1, 1997, Hong Kong comes under the rule of China. As such, Hong Kong's pivotal role as an economic link between Taiwan and China will soon shift to a different gear. The future relations between China, Taiwan and Hong Kong have become a subject of great interest and concern among policy makers and businessmen on both sides of the Taiwan Straits. I would like to share my thoughts with you on the relevant issues on this occasion. My speech today will be divided into three parts. First, I shall talk about China's economic performance and policies which will affect the future of Hong Kong and Taiwan. Then, I shall elaborate on the development of the economic relations between China, Taiwan and Hong Kong in recent years. The last part of my speech will focus on the possible development of these relations after 1997.

1. THE ECONOMIC PERFORMANCE AND POLICIES OF CHINA

China has been moving from a centrally planned economy toward a market economy since the economic reform measures taken by the government in 1978. It is pursuing a modified capitalist system with socialist characteristics, or the so-called «socialist market economy».

China's economy has experienced unprecedented growth and structural change since 1978. Real GDP growth averaged 9.8% throughout the 1980s and 11.9% in the first half of the 1990s. Since the economy showed signs of overheating in recent years, the authorities were compelled to adopt some cooling measures. A combination of administrative measures and tight fiscal and monetary policies brought the economy of China to a soft landing in 1996. Its real GDP grew 9.7% last year. Although down from 10.2% in 1995, the growth rate was still among the highest in the world. It is worth noting that the

---

[*] Senior Vice-President and Chief Economist, International Commercial Bank of China.

rapid economic growth in China was accompanied by further improvement in its external account and relative price stability. The current account surplus increased from US$1.2 billion in 1995 to US$1.6 billion in 1996. Inflation rate was cut by more than half from 14.8% in 1995 to 6.1% in 1996. This established an excellent beginning for the Ninth five-year Plan, 1996-2000.

Although China's economy has been enjoying a high rate of growth since the beginning of economic reforms in 1978 and its long-term development outlook is bright, it still faces a number of challenges, one of which is the vast gap between the coastal regions and the interior provinces. Other problems include unemployment and underemployment, increasing income inequality, infrastructure bottlenecks, food self-sufficiency, environmental problems, and the reform of state-owned enterprises. To meet these challenges, the Chinese government will need to maintain the momentum of its economic reforms. After the passing away of its paramount leader Deng Xiaoping, the Chinese government announced its intent to follow the course of Deng's policies on reform and openness. In my view, the economic reform of China has already crossed the point of no return.

In line with Deng Xiaoping's concept of «one country, two systems,» the Chinese government announced that Hong Kong will keep its current status as a Special Administrative Region according to the «Basic Law» for fifty years after its return. China's policies over Hong Kong will determine Hong Kong's future. Whether Hong Kong is going to play a leading role in the economy of southern China remains to be seen.

China has applied for membership in the World Trade Organisation (WTO), and in view of the size of its economy and trade volume, there is no doubt that China will be accepted as a member of the WTO. It is only a matter of time. In order to meet the prerequisites for joining the WTO, the Chinese government has announced concrete plans to adjust downward import tariffs and eliminate some tariff concessions on imported machinery and equipment. It has also reduced the rate of tax return from 14% to 9% for corporations producing and exporting raw materials. All these measures will certainly have an impact on the economies of both Hong Kong and Taiwan.

2. THE TRIANGULAR RELATIONSHIP BEFORE THE HANDOVER OF HONG KONG

China's relations with Hong Kong

The economic relationship between China and Hong Kong has been interdependent for a long time. It is attributable to two important factors. First, Hong Kong is adjacent to Guangdong province. Secondly, more than half of Hong Kong's native population is comprised of immigrants from Guangdong province. Due to their geographical proximity and shared ethnic origin, cross-border economic exchanges have prospered naturally.

Table 1: Hong Kong's Trade with China, (HK$ million)

	Domestic Exports	Re-exports	Total Exports	Imports	Total	Balance
1986	18,022	40,894	58,916	81,633	140,549	-22,717
1990	47,470	110,908	158,378	236,134	394,512	-77,756
1991	54,404	153,18	207,722	293,356	501,078	-85,634
1992	61,959	212,105	274,064	354,348	628,412	-80,284
1993	63,367	274,561	337,928	402,161	740,089	-64,233
1994	61,009	322,835	383,844	470,876	854,720	-87,032
1995	63,555	384,043	447,598	539,480	987,078	-91,882
1996	61,620	417,752	479,372	570,442	1.049,814	-91,070
1997Q1	12,863	95,488	108,351	129,267	237,618	-20,916

Source: *Hong Kong Monthly Digest of Statistics.*

In terms of trade, China was the largest export market for Hong Kong's domestic exports, amounting to HK$61,620 million in 1996 or 29% of total exports (see Table 1). China was also the most important supplier for the territory, providing HK$570,442 million, or 37% of Hong Kong's total imports. China depends on Hong Kong for its intermediary role with the economic world outside. Transhipment through Hong Kong to and from China has been brisk. In 1996, 57% of Hong Kong's re-exports to the world originated from China while 35% of its re-exports to China originated from the rest of the world.

Likewise, Hong Kong's dependence on China has been on the rise. In the past, Hong Kong relied on China for the supply of food and water, and from the 1980s onward, for cheap land and labor. According to rough estimates, Hong Kong enterprises have hired over 5 million workers in south-eastern China, a number greater than Hong Kong's entire labor force.

Hong Kong is the largest external investor in China. Its businessmen have invested US$100 billion in China (accounting for 70% of total foreign investment in China) and own $40 billion stocks in China-backed companies. Hong Kong businessmen own or operate 50,000 factories in Guangdong. As of the end of 1995, China's cumulative investments in Hong Kong totalled US$25 billion, making it the second largest foreign investor in Hong Kong. According to a report by Hang Seng Bank, the influence of China on Hong Kong's economy was nil before 1980, but in the span of ten years, China now accounts for 20% of Hong Kong's GDP.

For example, if direct investments by China in Hong Kong were halved in 1994, Hong Kong's GDP would have dropped 3.5%. If Hong Kong cut down its export processing activities in China by half, its GDP would go down by 1.4%. In short, Hong Kong depends more on China than China does on her.

Taiwan's Relations with Hong Kong

Now let us come to the relationship between Taiwan and Hong Kong. Both Taiwan and Hong Kong were included in the international system of division of labor in the 1950s. Since that time, they have both developed labor-intensive industries such as textiles, garments, shoes, and electronic products. Moreover, they both belong to the economic powerhouse known as the «Four Little Dragons,» which also include South Korea and Singapore. As such, they are more competitive than co-operative among themselves as far as economic development is concerned.

However, things have changed since China began its economic reforms in 1978. With the expansion of the market in the mainland and China's courtship of Taiwan, Hong Kong became an important intermediary for economic and trade exchanges between the two sides of the Taiwan Straits. Two-way trade between Hong Kong and Taiwan increased from US$1,801 million in 1980 to US$28,493 million in 1996 (see Table 2).

During the past five years, 1992-1996, the average annual growth of exports from Taiwan to Hong Kong was 14.9%, much higher than the average growth rate of 8.9% for Taiwan's total exports. Hong Kong has become the second largest export destination for Taiwan, amounting to US$26,788 million or 23.1% of total exports in 1996. At the same time, Taiwan imported US$1,705 million from Hong Kong, accounting for 1.7% of its total imports. Taiwan enjoyed a trade surplus of US$25,083 million, making Hong Kong the region from which Taiwan generated the most trade surplus.

This surplus resulted mainly from the easing of tensions between China and Taiwan, through Hong Kong's role as the entrepot for trade between both sides of the Taiwan Straits. According to the statistics of the Hong Kong government, transhipment through Hong Kong for trade between China and Taiwan increased from US$78 million in 1979 to US$1,516 million in 1987 and to US$11,300 million in 1996 (see Table 3).

Table 2: Taiwan's Trade with Hong Kong (US$ million)

	Exports	Imports	Total	Balance
1979	1,140	205	1,345	+935
1980	1,551	250	1,801	+1,301
1985	2,540	320	2,860	+2,220
1990	8,556	1,446	10,002	+7,110
1991	1,.431	1,947	14,378	+10,484
1992	15,415	1,781	17,196	+13,634
1993	18,453	1,729	20,182	+16,724
1994	21,262	1,533	22,795	+19,729
1995	26,106	1,843	27,949	+24,263
1996	26,788	1,705	28,493	+25,083
1997 Jan.-May	10,913	769	11,682	+10,144

Source: Council for Economic Planning and Development, Taiwan *Statistical Data Book, 1996.*

Trade between both sides of the Taiwan Straits through Hong Kong as a percentage of the two-way trade between Hong Kong and Taiwan increased from 5% in 1979 to 40% in 1990 and to 56% in 1996.

With regard to trade interdependence between Hong Kong and Taiwan, Taiwan's trade with Hong Kong as a percentage of its total trade with the world rose from 5.2% in 1986 to 13.1% in 1996. Similarly, Hong Kong's trade with Taiwan as a percentage of its total trade with the world increased from 2.1% to 5.3% during the same period. Taiwan has emerged as the fourth largest trading partner of Hong Kong while Hong Kong has become Taiwan's third largest trading partner.

Taiwan also has considerable investments in Hong Kong. According to official statistics, the amount of approved investment rose from US$1.3 million (for 3 cases) in 1987 to about US$200 million (for 49 cases) in 1991 and then decreased to about US$60 million (for 37 cases) in 1996 (see Table 4).

Table 3: Hong Kong's Trade with Taiwan (US$ million)

	Import from Taiwan		Export to Taiwan		Total Trade with Taiwan		
	Total	Of which: re-export to China	Total	Of Which: re-export originated from China	Total	Of which: re-export to and from China	% of total
1979	1,207.0	21.5	346.0	56.3	1,553.0	778	5.0
1980	1,592.2	235.0	445.8	76.2	2,038.0	311.2	15.3
1985	2,679.2	986.9	554.5	115.9	3,233.7	1,102.7	34.1
1987	4,274.0	1,226.5	1,241.7	288.9	5,515.7	1,515.5	27.5
1990	7,446.7	3,278.3	2,724.1	765.4	10,170.8	4,043.6	39.8
1991	9,563.0	4,667.2	3,175.0	1,126.0	12,738.0	5,793.1	45.5
1992	11,301.2	6,287.9	3,396.9	1,119.0	14,698.1	7,406.9	50.4
1993	12,203.7	7,585.4	3,658.6	1,103.6	15,862.3	8,689.0	54.8
1994	13,936.3	8,517.2	3,700.3	1,292.3	17,636.6	9,809.5	55.6
1995	16,572.6	9,882.8	4,580.6	1,574.2	21,153.2	11,457.0	57.9
1996	15,795.1	9,717.6	4,274.8	1,582.4	20,069.9	11,300.0	56.3

Note: The figures contained in this table are not comparable to those shown in
Table 2 due to differences in valuation, scope and timing.
Source: Mainland Affairs Council, Taipei, Taiwan, ROC.

From 1952 to May 1997, the accumulated investments in Hong Kong totalled US$866 million for 384 cases. It was estimated that around 8,000 Taiwanese firms opened subsidiaries in Hong Kong through which they channelled investment into China. In the meantime, Hong Kong invested US$2.65 billion for 1,773 cases in Taiwan. Hong Kong has become one of the major sources of foreign investment in Taiwan.

Taiwan's Relations with China

In 1978, China began advocating doing business with Taiwan by way of Hong Kong and Macau. The next year, it called for «exchanges of commerce, communication, and transportation» between the two sides of the Taiwan Straits in its «Letter to the Taiwanese Compatriots». In 1980-1982, China announced that it would regard doing business with Taiwan as domestic business and hence exempt it from the levy of customs duties.

In a similar friendly move, Taiwan lifted the ban on its citizens to visit China in November 1987. Taiwan also relaxed rules forbidding its businessmen to invest in China. While retaining a ban on direct commerce, communication, and transportation, it presented a leeway for all Taiwan-China related business to be conducted through a third country; therefore, Hong Kong became a vital intermediary in this bilateral trade.

Since 1978, China's open door policy and its establishment of special economic zones have provided investors with a most convenient and logical venue for diversifying their production bases. In recent years, China has become the most favoured overseas investment destination for Taiwan enterprises due to the following factors: same ethnic roots, inexpensive work force and land, rich natural resources, and huge market potential. Taiwan enterprises are also driven to China by the exodus of plants in related industrial sectors. All the while, Hong Kong has been an important base for Taiwan's investors interested in China since October 1990.

Table 4: Taiwan's Approved Foreign and Overseas Chinese investment to and from Hong Kong (US$ million).

	Hong Kong's Investment in Taiwan		Taiwan's Investment In Hong Kong	
	Case	Amount (US million)	Case	Amount (US million)
1952-1986	1,157	611.6	13	8.4
1987	63	181.3	3	1.3
1988	75	156.8	9	8.1
1989	65	248.2	5	10.4
1990	69	236.0	27	33.1
1991	58	128.6	49	199.6
1992	68	213.0	53	·54.4
1993	53	169.3	79	161.9
1994	48	250.7	47	127.3
1995	37	146.6	50	99.6
1996	57	266.9	37	59.9
1997, Jan-May	23	43.7	12	101.6
1952-May 1997	1,773	2,652.6	384	865.5

Source: Investment Commission, Ministry of Economic Affairs, Taipei, Taiwan, ROC.

Over the past few years, Taiwan's indirect investment in China increased drastically. According to the statistics released by the Ministry of Economic Affairs of the ROC, the approved indirect investment in China by Taiwanese firms through Hong Kong amounted to US$7.3 billion for 11,823 cases during the period 1991-May 1997 (see Table 5).

These figures are much lower than those released by the Chinese authorities. The official statistics by the Chinese authorities indicated that as of March 1996 there were 32,800 Taiwan-invested enterprises in China with a total capital of US$11.9 billion, accounting for 8.4% of all foreign investment. This value made Taiwan the second largest foreign capital supplier to China, next only to Hong Kong. Other informal estimates have put the total amount of Taiwan investment at around US$30 billion, with direct employment of five million workers.

Table 5: Approved Indirect Investment in China, 1991-May 1997

	Case	Amount (US$ million)
1991	237	174.2
1992	264	247.0
1993	9,329	3,168.4
1994	934	962.2
1995	490	1,092.7
1996	383	1,229.2
1997, Jan.-May	186	390.3
1991-May 1997	11,823	7,264.0

Source: Investment Commission, Ministry of Economic Affairs, Taiwan, and ROC.

Investments from Taiwan and Hong Kong have provided capital, advanced technology and managerial skills to China, which have contributed greatly to the economic reform and modernisation of China in the past years. It has also promoted economic co-operation among Taiwan, Hong Kong and southern China, particularly in Guangdong and Fujian provinces, otherwise known as the Southern China Growth Triangle. Unlike other growth triangles formed mostly out of the deliberate initiatives of governments, the growth triangle among China, Taiwan and Hong Kong is a market and private sector-driven arrangement.

As mentioned in the section on Taiwan's relations with Hong Kong, cross-Straits trade has increased rapidly, rising from US$78 million in 1979 to US$1,516 million in 1987 and to US$11,300 million in 1996 (see Table 6).

Table 6: Bilateral Trade Between Taiwan and China (US$million)

	Taiwan Exports to China		Taiwan Imports from China		Total	Balance
	Amount	% of total Exports	Amount	% of total Imports		
1979	22	0.1	56	0.4	78	-34
1981	384	1.7	75	0.4	459	+309
1987	1,227	2.3	289	0.8	1,516	+938
1988	2,242	3.7	479	1.0	2,721	+1,763
1989	2,896	4.4	587	1.1	3,483	+2,309
1990	3,278	4.9	765	1.4	4,043	+2,513
1991	4,667	6.1	1,126	1.8	5,793	+3,541
1992	6,288	7.7	1,119	1.6	7,407	+5,169
1993	7,585	8.9	1,104	1.4	8,689	+6,481
1994	8,517	9.2	1,292	1.5	9,809	+7,225
1995	9,883	8.9	1,574	1.5	11,457	+8,309
1996	9,718	8.4	1,582	1.6	11,300	+8,136

Source: Industry of Free China, May 1997.

The trade volume across the Taiwan Straits increased about 6.5 times in less than ten years. The degree of trade dependence also increased steadily on both sides

Taiwan's trade dependence on China rose from 1.1% in 1981 to about 11% in 1996, while China's dependence on Taiwan increased from 1% to 8.2% during the same period. Taiwan depended less on China than China depended on Taiwan before 1992. However, the trend reversed after that year, and the rate exceeded 10% in 1994. Taiwan was concerned about the trend of ever-increasing dependence on China's resources and markets. Taiwan government faces the dilemma of whether or not to further give in to the comparative advantages that China can offer (see table 7).

Table 7: Mutual Trade Dependence, Taiwan and China (%)

	Taiwan on China	China on Taiwan
1981	1.05	1.04
1987	1.71	2.06
1990	4.23	4.47
1991	6.20	6.35
1992	7.60	7.05
1993	9.32	7.71
1994	10.02	7.55
1995	10.46	8.02
1996	10.95	8.21

Source: Mainland Affairs Council, Taipei, Taiwan, ROC.

It is worth noting that in May 1997, the governments of both China and Taiwan gave approval for shipping companies on either side of the Taiwan Straits to carry freight from a preauthorized port on one side (Kaohsiung) to a preauthorized port on the other side (Fuzhou and Xiamen). This signifies a vital breakthrough in the long stagnant cross-Straits economic relations, making it possible for Taiwan to implement a series of follow-up liberalisation measures. After the inauguration of an offshore transhipping center in Kaohsiung, a warehousing and transhipment zone will be established. Following that, direct transportation links across the Taiwan Straits is anticipated.

From November 1987, when Taiwan lifted the ban on its citizens to visit China, to January 1997, more than 1.7 million of Taiwan's citizens have visited China (see Table 8).

Table 8: Visit between People of Taiwan and China (number of people)

	Taiwanese Visitors to China	Chinese Visitors to Taiwan
1987	6,905	28,00
1988	223,647	381,00
1989	188,372	4,838
1990	70,395	7,520
1991	14,350	11,074
1992	8,141	13,134
1993	384,081	18,343
1994	413,026	23,562
1995	327,387	42,634
1996	109,739	58,010
1997- Jan.	4,226	6,273
1987-Jan.1997	1,750,269	185,797

Source: Ministry of Interior, Taipei, Taiwan, and ROC.

The purposes of their visits have included meeting friends and relatives, doing business, and sightseeing. On the other hand, as of January 1997, 185,797 Chinese residents have visited Taiwan. It may be noted that the figures are underestimated. The growing people-to-people association has strengthened mutual understanding and relations.

3. THE TRIANGULAR RELATIONSHIP AFTER THE HANDOVER OF HONG KONG

China's Relations with Hong Kong

After the return of Hong Kong to the sovereignty of China at midnight on June 30, 1997, the very element that has made Hong Kong the stepping-stone to China-Taiwan links will no longer exist. Hong Kong is going to become an integral part of China proper. As the governments of China and Taiwan wrangle about the legitimacy of the representation of China, businessmen on both sides of the Taiwan Straits are waiting to see what will become of the Hong Kong leg of the lucrative triangle. What is more, Hong Kong residents will wonder what will become of their future.

Politically, the Sino-British Joint Declaration governing the future of Hong Kong is an international document registered with the United Nations, so it stands to reason that China will try to honor this international obligation to the fullest degree. The Joint Declaration provides that Hong Kong's social and economic systems and lifestyle will remain unchanged, that rights and freedom enjoyed by the people of Hong Kong will be preserved, and that features of the capitalist system such as private property, ownership of enterprises and the right of inheritance and foreign investment will be protected.

As guaranteed by the Basic Law, Hong Kong is supposed to enjoy a high degree of autonomy. In spite of this, what happens to Hong Kong will be closely watched by the people of Taiwan. China promises «one country, two systems» for the government and people of Taiwan in its attempts to woo Taiwan for its consent to reunification. However, this policy is applicable only to the economic system, and not to the political system. The Chinese authorities have no intention of allowing a fully democratic system in Hong Kong. If China fails to abide by her promise to Hong Kong, she will run the risk of forcing Taiwan to seek independence and separate itself from China

The economic importance of Hong Kong to China is vital. China is most likely to try every means possible to maintain the economic prosperity and stability of Hong Kong after July 1, 1997. Many more Chinese firms will open branches in Hong Kong, making it no longer necessary for foreign businessmen to go to China to do business. On the other hand, Hong Kong, as a Special Administrative Region of China, will be in a position to make significant contributions to the modernisation of China, particularly in the areas of trade, finance, commerce, business management, social development, democracy and the legal system.   In the long run, the policy of the Hong Kong Special Administrative Region government and the Hong Kong-China relationship under the Basic Law will determine whether the favourable business environment will be affected by the changing circumstances of civil and political rights, increasing social and economic inequality, and so on and so forth.

Taiwan's Relations with Hong Kong

The Taiwanese authorities anticipate that the handover of Hong Kong is not going to affect the economic exchange and trade between Taiwan and Hong Kong. In June 1995, Qian Qichen, China's Vice-Premier and Foreign Minister announced seven basic principles governing Beijing's handling of Hong Kong's relations with Taiwan after 1997. Qian's seven points guaranteed that existing non-government exchanges between Hong Kong and Taiwan will not be affected.

As mentioned before, prior to the opening up of China, Hong Kong had long served as the only gateway for its trade with the rest of the world. After the handover, Hong Kong will remain the most important door through which business is done with the rest of the world. As a result, unless direct sailing between China and Taiwan materialises, Hong Kong's role as an entrepot for trade between the two sides of the Taiwan Straits is expected to continue. However, official contacts between Taiwan and Hong Kong will have to go by way of Beijing. Consequently, Hong Kong is likely to play a more significant intermediary role in the future relationship between Taiwan and China.

In light of the aforementioned developments, I shall cite a few examples to bear this out. First, Taiwan has reiterated on different occasions that all of its agencies in Hong Kong will remain in place in whatever appropriate forms after the handover. Secondly, Taiwan and Hong Kong recently solved the question of flag flying for ships travelling between Hong Kong and Taiwan, and concluded the sea link talks satisfactorily. Thirdly, both sides agreed last year to extend the air agreement for another five years, thus honouring it to well beyond 1997. There will be no disruption of Taiwan's trade with and via Hong Kong in the future.

In short, as long as Hong Kong maintains its democratic system, Taiwan will also maintain its direct trade, investment, air and sea links, free movement of people, goods and capital, and other existent connections with Hong Kong. Under these circumstances, the relationship between Taiwan and Hong Kong will remain unchanged in the future.

Taiwan's Relations with China

The economic relations between Taiwan and China are expected to improve in the coming years. However, the economic links cannot alleviate or offset the existing political tensions between them. The relationship between Taiwan and China has been strained since President Lee Teng-hui visited Cornell University in 1995 and won his presidency in March 1996. China conducted military exercises and missile tests before the presidential election in an attempt to intimidate the people in Taiwan. In retaliation to Taiwan's pragmatic diplomacy, China has used every means possible to isolate Taiwan from the international community and block Taiwan from developing official relations with countries that have diplomatic ties with China. Consequently, Taiwan government has urged businessmen to carefully review their investment in China to «avoid hastiness» and has cautioned them to «use restraint» in making heavy investments in China. Those entrepreneurs investing in China without government consent will be fined. A new list of prohibited investment areas has been drawn up; these sectors include infrastructure, high technology, defence and finance.

At present, all quasi-official and indirect contacts between the two sides through the Straits Exchange Foundation and the Association for Relations across the Taiwan Straits have been suspended until the «weather» in the Taiwan Straits becomes clear. In an interview with the Washington Times in June 1997, President Lee Teng-hui urged Beijing to abandon its hegemonic attitude in handling cross-Straits relations. He called for resumption of formal dialogue so that the wide-ranging problems between Taiwan and China can be pragmatically resolved on the basis of parity. Taiwan government authorities regard Beijing's «one country, two systems» scheme unfit as a model for Chinese reunification since the Hong Kong model is not in accord with the wishes of the people in Taiwan. Taipei also urged Beijing to give up the use of military force as a means of national reunification.

In addition to the astounding rate of increase in cross-Straits interactions and exchanges in recent years, there are still opportunities and areas for economic co-operation on both sides of the Taiwan Straits. The economies of China, Taiwan and Hong Kong are complementary to each other. The comparative advantages of these three economies are distinct. China has rich natural resources and an abundant supply of land and trainable labor. Taiwan has an abundance of capital, and its technological capability surpasses both China and Hong Kong in technology-intensive industries. Hong Kong has time-honoured experience in financial and commercial services, ample capital and an abundance of entrepreneurs. In addition to economic complementarities, China, Taiwan and Hong Kong are geographically proximate and share cultural affinities. With their comparative advantages, the Southern China Growth

Triangle has been formed, mainly driven by mutual needs and initiatives from the private sector. Great potential for further co-operation still exists among these three economies since most of their complementarities have yet to be exploited. Even though they have different political and economic systems, the formation of a greater China economic bloc would be for the benefit of all.

4. CONCLUSION

The intimate and mutually rewarding economic relationship between Hong Kong and China has developed rapidly since China opened its door to the rest of the world in 1978. There is no doubt that the transformation of the Chinese economy in the last two decades has contributed enormously to the growth and diversification of Hong Kong's economy. At the same time, Hong Kong's role as a service and marketing center, its global network of commercial and trading relationships, and its large core of professionals will provide expertise, managerial skills and effective infrastructure, thereby contributing to China's modernisation in the 21st century.

The economic relationship between Hong Kong and China after the handover is expected to broaden and deepen during the honeymoon period. However, their long-term economic relations will depend on Beijing's attitude and policy toward Hong Kong. The «one country, two systems» policy will not work if the Chinese authorities put political principles above the management of the Hong Kong economy. Moreover, if economic freedom and market openness cannot be preserved, it will be impossible for Hong Kong to maintain continuous stability and prosperity in the coming years.

At present, there exists a discrepancy in cross-Straits relations. Their economic relations seem to be co-operative and complementary, but their political relations are competitive and confrontational. With regard to future prospects for economic relations between Taiwan and China, there is a challenge for leadership in both Taipei and Beijing to open up channels of communication, improve mutual understanding and trust, increase bilateral trade and investment, and explore areas of economic co-operation for the benefit of the people on both sides of the Taiwan Straits.

Regarding future political relations between Taiwan and China, President Lee Teng-hui expressed his wish to undertake a journey of peace to China to meet with President Jiang Zemin in his presidential inaugural address in May 1996. There is no doubt that the exchange of visits between these two top leaders will break the ice between Taiwan and China and lessen hostility in the Taiwan Straits. Over time, mutually beneficial and complementary relations are expected to develop. The improvement in bilateral relations between Taiwan and China should foster peace and stability in the Asia-Pacific region.

BIBLIOGRAPHY

Chen, Edward K.Y., February 1993, *Southern China Growth Triangle*, paper presented at a workshop on Growth Triangles in Asia, Asian Development Bank, Manila, Philippines.

Cheng, Joseph Y.S., May 1997, *Towards the Establishment of a New Order,* paper presented at an international conference on «The Hong Kong Handover and its Implications», Taipei, Taiwan, ROC.

Chung-Hua Institution for Economic Research, April 1997, various papers presented at the Seminar on Economic Development in Mainland China, Taipei, Taiwan, and ROC.

Klintworth, Gary, May 1997, *Hong Kong's Return to Chinese Sovereignty: The Strategic Implications,* paper presented at an international conference on «The Hong Kong Handover and its Implications», Taipei, Taiwan, ROC.

Ming, Chu-Cheng, May 1997, *«The Republic of China's Mainland Policy Beyond 1997,»* paper presented at an international conference on «The Hong Kong Handover and its Implications», Taipei, Taiwan, ROC.

CHINA RISING: DEVELOPMENT ISSUES AND OPTIONS FOR THE 21st CENTURY

Vikram NEHRU*

Reaching conclusions on Chinese development issues and options for the 21st century is difficult because these issues are very wide ranging and the possible discussion about them is fascinating.

But China is always fascinating. It is fascinating because the country is so unusual, with its 5000-year history, its huge size, its impenetrable language, and the complexity of its current situation.

The complexity of its current situation arises from the fact that the country is undergoing two transitions. The first transition is from a rural agricultural society to an urban industrial one. The second transition is from a command economy to a market based one. The interplay and synergy between these two transitions have sparked very rapid growth and what is all remarkable about it, is that it is in a country which is equivalent in size to all of Africa and all of Latin america taken together.

This is a triumph not just for the Chinese; it is a triumph for humanity because 200 million people have been raised out of poverty in this country over the last 17 years. At the same time however, the confluence of these two transitions, has created new problems, new challenges. Six main advantages can be presented together with five major challenges.

The strengths of the Chinese economy

China's rapid growth can largely be explained by these strengths and advantages.

Most important have been high savings as mentioned in Mr Wing Thye Woo's presentation about the growth of capital stock.

* Principal Economist, China and Mongolia Department, World Bank.

There are the advantages of backwardness. There is a large amount of surplus labour, available in agriculture, which is transferred to relatively, high productivity manufacturing, which stimulates growth.

One of the impressive legacies of the Maoist era, is the relatively literacy of the labour force. For a country at this level of per capita income, China has a labour force which is more literate than in other developing countries.

China is relatively stable. Again, given the ups and downs of the economy, there has been more stability in China than in many other developing countries, especially those in Latin America and in Africa.

China has administrative strength, which goes back not just over the past few decades, but for centuries, if not millennia. There are examples of Chinese administrative strength which go all the way back to the beginning of this millennium.

Finally, China has a huge Diaspora of Chinese who have been willing to invest in the country, now that it has opened up its economy.

The challenges

These strengths are well known but there are enormous challenges which China has to face which, who knows, may prove to be overwhelming.

The foremost challenge is the challenge of incomplete transition. The fact is that China is midway in its transition to a market based economy. Its state enterprise sector is only partly reformed. Its financial sector is very fragile, and there are many examples around the world of how financial sectors with such enormous fragility have collapsed with major consequences for growth.

China has a rapidly deteriorating environment. The fact is that rapid economic growth and rapid urbanisation have created enormous problems in air pollution, in water pollution in acid rain and have also led to environmental degradation in agriculture.

China faces income insecurity. By income insecurity we mean the bracing effects of competition have led to the greater likelihood of unemployment, of having to move jobs, of moving from village to town to city. Migration is becoming a daily phenomenon now in China. From a small trickle of migrants in the 80's, it is now become a huge flood of migrants to the cities, and within cities, more and more workers have to leave state enterprises to join non-state enterprises, as the non-state enterprise sector has been expanding much faster, and the state sector is facing financial problems.

In addition of course, there are problems with the elderly, those who had pensions available to them from the state sector. Now with the problems in the state sector the pensions are no longer forthcoming. In rural areas this has been a big problem for the old. But the number of old in China is increasing very rapidly. This is a demographic transition, that is taking place in the economy.

Inequality is rising. Large disparities have occurred between provinces and what is unusual about China is that it's huge rising inequality is actually unprecedented. We do not know any other country in the last 40 years, which has had such a rapid rise in inequality. Inequality tends to be stable in these countries over time. China is exceptional in that regard, but it went from a relatively egalitarian society to a reasonably unequal society now. We can say "reasonably" because our estimates suggest that China is now more unequal than many transition economies. It is about as unequal as United States but it is less unequal than many countries in Latin America and Asia.

However, what is interesting to note is that regional inequality contributes relatively little to the aggregate inequality in China, according to our estimates, the bulk of inequality stems from rural/urban income differences, even within provinces, not between provinces.

Food shortages. This is a very odd thing to write about because, actually, China has enormous surpluses of grain. But food shortages are concern Chinese leaders have. They face the task of feeding, a fifth of the world's population, with only 7% of arable land in the world and this, together with concerns about frictions with trading partners in the world economy, has led them to the concern about agricultural self-sufficiency. The danger here is that China will propel itself down a path, along with some other East-Asian countries of developing high cost agriculture, behind high protection barriers. However this is a costly path which a developing country, like China, cannot perhaps afford. So this is definitely an issue confronting the country.

Last is the problem of possible frictions, for a country the size of China, which is developing its exports as rapidly as it, has been doing. This has created frictions with its trading countries and is also leading to some concerns in competitor countries, with similar levels of comparative advantage, countries like India for example, or Indonesia.

Towards 2020

With so many challenges and such strong advantages, it is a bold man indeed who wants to predict about the future of the country. Certainly, the World Bank has not been very good about predicting or projecting China's growth in the past, but oddly enough, unlike in other countries, where we have constantly over projected growth (in other words where reality has always come out at a lower level than we projected), in China we have consistently under projected growth. And there is a danger that we might do this in the future as well, so rather than try and predict or project any single growth rate, what we have tried to do this time is to give a range of possible outcomes, along two different dimensions: saving rates and Total Factor Productivity (TFP) growth rate.

Capital accumulation and efficiency improvements have been the two key factors in explaining Chinese growth, so we have taken these two key factors and we have asked what is likely to happen if we use different numbers for each. With a combination of a 20% savings rate and a 1% TFP growth rate, growth rises by 4.2% a year for the next 25 years, or it can go up to 7.9 -8%, with 40% savings and a 3% total factor productivity. In other words, a very wide range is possible. China's saving rate is now about 40%, so getting a growth rate of 6.4% per year with a 1% TFP growth rate is very probable.

There is a concern that China's saving rate may actually decline in the future. It may decline because of the rapidly ageing population for example. But there are many forces within China which argue for a rising saving rate. Simply, the fact that there is more market force now is encouraging people to save. There are great uncertainties for which households have to save. There is the fear of unemployment, the desire for a house, a concern about aged parents and so forth which drive people to save a lot more. How these two forces work out is difficult to know. Some groups have suggested the saving's rate is likely to decline, and a recent article by Sachs *and alii*, as well as report from the Asian Development Bank have suggested that the saving's rate is likely to decline.

But let's take a growth rate of 6.7% of GDP, for the next 25 years, what does it mean? Obviously right now growth is much higher than that, and growth is likely to decline over time. Abstracting from cycles, talking here about long term trends, the growth rate is likely to decline to 5.5 % by the year 2020.

There are three reasons for this.

The labour force will stop growing around the period era 2000 to 2015, because of the demographics of China, its one child policy and its rapidly ageing population.

With rising capital stocks, the marginal productivity of capital would be expected to decline.

As China's per capita income rises, its ability to catch up with the rest of the world will decline. So we expect basically a declining GDP growth rate over time and if we take the 6.7% as the point of reference, then by the year 2020 it will be around 5 to 5.5%. One of the reasons why this is an interesting number is that this is very close to the long-term forecast of the Chinese themselves.

And what does all this mean for policy?

In the past, under a command economy, the government was able to determine the saving's rate because it adjusted prices. State enterprises made higher profits or lower profits, as the case may have been, and these profits were transferred to the government and then they were used for the investments. But now, in a market economy, things are much more indirect, and the two most important inputs under the policy process are that of reforms and stability, and the way they affect households and enterprises. The combination of these two effects on households and enterprises are going to lead to efficiency gains, in the form of TFP growth and higher savings, and the combination of these two will progressively lead to higher growth. In other words, if you have high savings and low TFP growth you could end up at the same level of growth rate. So this is a sort of broad conceptual basis which underlines the models that we used.

What does this mean by 2020?

Somebody mentioned that China could be the largest economy in the world. We have taken a somewhat different view. In terms of per capita income, which we think is the more appropriate measure, and if you look at China today, in PPP terms (PPP US dollars) with 6.7% growth as in the last scenario, China will be about where Portugal is today, and less than half as much as the US is today in year 2020. That gives us some idea of the kind of standard of living that China could be seeing in the year 2020, provided of course it gets over its major problem of the environment, because such a growth rate could actually lead to huge environmental problems if they go unchecked. The sector growth underpinning this particular scenario entails a relatively high agricultural growth rate. But we think that this actually could occur because of government's renewing interest in agriculture, following the announcement of the ninth five-year plan. And China has consistently had agricultural growth rates over 4%, so it is not unusual by historical standards.

But the more interesting issue is what this kind of growth rate will do to the structure of the labour force, because what this means is a huge change in the way people work, more importantly where they work. What we are obviously projecting is a substantial increase in the allocation of labour to services and industry. This big shift implies roughly 200 million people moving out of agriculture, a massive outflow, with implications for migration, for urbanisation, for social unrest which are fantastic and can be underestimated. It is in fact what is at the back of the minds of all Chinese policy makers, when they talk about change, talk about the pace of growth, talk about concerns of labour mobility and so forth. And it really points the very heart of the complexity which underlies what is happening in China and what is likely to happen in China: a very uncertain future. A future full of promise, but a future filled with dangers, because in a country of 1.2 billion people (soon 1.4 billion people by the year 2020) where the number of elderly doubles (so the share of elderly doubles from 6% of the population to 12 % of the population) these are large changes demographically, large changes in employment structure, in the location of labour. Whenever they deal with any policy issue, whether it is straight liberalisation or just the opening up of the financial sector, whether it is liberalisation of state enterprises or privatisation, the Chinese policy makers are aware of all the dangers they may have to face in the future.

The Authors[1]

ERIC BOUTEILLER
Deputy Director of the Eurasia Institute, (Ecole des Hautes Etudes Commerciales-Paris), in charge of the studies regarding the Chinese world. Recent publications include *Les Nouveaux empereurs, l'apogée du capitalisme chinois*, Paris : Calman-Lévy, 1997.

ANDRE CHIENG
Chairman, Asiatique européenne de commerce, Paris, trade and consulting company specialized in China (société de commerce et de conseil spécialisée sur la Chine) ; Vice-President of the France-China Committee of the CNPF (France's Employers Confederation). Economic adviser to the Government of the Hebei district (China) in 1988.

JEAN-LUC DOMENACH
Scientific Director at the Fondation Nationale des Sciences Politiques, where he was the Director of the Centre d'Etudes et de Recherches Internationales (CERI) from 1985 to 1994. Recent books include *Chine : l'Archipel oublié*, Paris : Fayard, 1992.

ALAIN DUTHEIL
Chairman, ST.Microelectronics. He joined Texas Instruments in 1969, then Thomson Semiconducteurs in 1983. Appointed Corporate Vice-President, Strategic Planning in May 1994, in addition to his positions as Corporate Vice-President, Human Resources and President & Chief Executive Officer of SGS-Thomson Microelectronic SA (France).

MICHEL FOUQUIN
Deputy Director of the CEPII, Associate Professor at the University of Paris I-la Sorbonne, specialized in international trade issues and the development of Asian NIC's, co-author of *Le développement économique de l'Asie orientale*, La Découverte, Paris, 1995.

FAN GANG
Director of the National Institute of Economic Research attached to the China Reform Foundation (Beijing) ; professor of economics at the Graduate School of the Chinese Academy of Social Sciences. Consultant for various departments of the Chinese central government, as well as for international organizations. Recent books include *Market Mechanism and Economic Efficiency*, Shanghaï University Press, 1993.

---

[1] As off June 1997.

FRANÇOISE LEMOINE
Senior economist at the CEPII. Specialized on the economics of the transition in the East European countries and in China, with a focus on the integration of these countries in the world economy. Among her publications : coeditor of *Different Paths to a Market Economy:China and European Economies in Transition*, published by the Development Centre, OECD (1998).

GEORGE S.K. LEUNG
Economic adviser at the Hongkong Bank which he joined in 1994 as a senior economist with the economic research department. Before joining the Bank, he held several positions, in the private sector as well as in the public sector where he was senior adviser with the Department of the Treasury (State of Victoria, Australia).

ANGUS MADDISON
Professor of Economics at the University of Groningen; he has held various academic positions such as at the Center for International Affairs (Harvard University, 1969-1971), the Nuffield College (1975) and the St Antony's college (1988) at the Oxford University.   Consultant for several international organizations, one of his recent publication is *Explaining the Economic Performance of Nations : Essays in Time and Space* (1995).

VIKRAM NEHRU
Principal economist, China and Mongolia Department, the World Bank. After four years with the government of India, he joined the World Bank in 1981, where he worked on countries like Indonesia, Malaysia, Nigeria, Ghana and China. Author of several articles in academic journals and of World Bank reports, including issues of *Global Economic Prospects and the Developing Countries.*

SAMUEL PINTO
Deputy Director General, having begun his career at Paribas, he become director of the private investment management department with Crédit Agricole in Hong Kong (1989-1992). He is presently responsible for the insitutional management of stocks and rates, working on strategic investment.

RUOEN REN
Professor at the School of Management, Beijing University of Aeronautics and Astronautics. His research work focuses on providing an internationally comparable measure of the Chinese economy.

VINCENT DE RIVAZ
Executive Vice President, International Division, EDF since March 1995. Former Director of the Far East Region in this division (1989-1991), he was particularly responsible for the development of EDF in China which he initiated in 1985, and also for the development of the company in Japan, Taiwan and Korea.

ADAM SZIRMAI
Professor of development studies at the Department of Technology and Development Studies, University of Technology, Eindhoven, since 1994, and research fellow at the School of Management (Beijing, April 1996). Included among his numerous publications written on China, since 1988 with Ren Ruoen, is "Assessing Growth Rates in China", in *Trade Policies and Trade Patterns during Transition : a Comparison between China and the CEECs*, OECD Development Centre, (1998).

HEH-SONG WANG
Senior Vice-President and Chief Economist at the International Commercial Bank of China after having held various positions at the Central Bank of China (Taipei). Professor of Economics at the Fu-Jen Catholic University, Tapei (1996-1997), and at the Graduate Institute of Southeast Asian Studies, Tamkang University, Taipei, since March 1997.

WING THYE WOO
Professor, Department of Economics, University of California, Davis. Consultant on macroeconomics and exchange rate management, trade issues and financial sector development for various international organizations and governments, the Chinese government; he recently published " Dynamic Growth in China : Lessons in Economic Reforms for other Developing Countries ", in *Economic Reforms : Inter-Country Experiences and Lessons for India*, Mac Millan press, 1998.

Imprimé en France. – JOUVE, 18, rue Saint-Denis, 75001 PARIS
N° 259830K. Dépôt légal : Août 1998